A Guide to
Spiritual Discernment

A Guide to Spiritual Discernment

Compiled by
Bishop Rueben P. Job

Foreword by
Marjorie J. Thompson

Cover Design: Steve Laughbaum
Interior Design and Layout: Nancy Cole
First Printing: September 1996

Printed in the United States of America

Library of Congress Cataloging-in-Publication Data

Job, Rueben P.
    A guide to spiritual discernment / Rueben P. Job.
      p.   cm.
    ISBN 0-8358-0779-7
    1. Discernment of spirits—Prayer-books and devotions—English.
2. Spiritual life—Christianity. 3. Christian life—Methodist authors.
4. Devotional calendars.   I. Title.
BV5083.J63   1996   96-14994
248.3—dc20   CIP

*For those
who first and always
seek God's will*

Contents

Acknowledgments

The publisher gratefully acknowledges permission to reproduce the following copyrighted material:

John W. Bardsley, Meditation for September 16 in *Upper Room Disciplines 1995.* (Nashville: Upper Room Books, 1994). Used by permission of the publisher.

George W. Bashore, Meditation for April 16 in *Upper Room Disciplines 1994.* (Nashville: Upper Room Books, 1993). Used by permission of the publisher.

Keith Beasley-Topliffe: From "If Thine Eye Be Single" in *Weavings: A Journal of the Christian Spiritual Life*, Vol. VIII, No. 3, May/June 1993. (Nashville: The Upper Room, 1993). Used by permission of the author.

Michel Bouttier, *Prayers for My Village*, trans. by Lamar Williamson. (Nashville: Upper Room Books, 1994). Used by permission of the publisher.

José P. Bové, Meditation for January 18 in *Upper Room Disciplines 1994.* (Nashville: Upper Room Books, 1993). Used by permission of the publisher.

Charles R. Brown, Meditation for October 4 in *Upper Room Disciplines 1994.* (Nashville: Upper Room Books, 1993). Used by permission of the publisher.

Minerva G. Carcaño, Meditation for July 14 in *Upper Room Disciplines 1993.* (Nashville: Upper Room Books, 1992). Used by permission of the publisher.

Judith Freeman Clark, Meditations for March 7, 10 in *Upper Room Disciplines 1995.* (Nashville: Upper Room Books, 1994). Used by permission of the publisher.

John Clifford, Meditations for April 9, 10 in *Upper Room Disciplines 1994.* (Nashville: Upper Room Books, 1993). Used by permission of the publisher.

William Sloane Coffin, "An Interview with William Sloane Coffin" in *Alive Now*, May/June 1993. (Nashville: The Upper Room, 1993). Used by permission of the author.

Judith Craig, Meditation for October 11 in *Upper Room Disciplines 1995.* (Nashville: Upper Room Books, 1994). Used by permission of the publisher.

Hilda R. Davis, Meditation for September 6 in *Upper Room Disciplines 1995.* (Nashville: Upper Room Books, 1994). Used by permission of the publisher.

Gerrit S. Dawson, Meditation for July 30 in *Upper Room Disciplines 1994.* (Nashville: Upper Room Books, 1993). Used by permission of the publisher.

Esther de Waal, Meditations for January 17, 20 in *Upper Room Disciplines 1995.* (Nashville: Upper Room Books, 1994). Used by permission of the publisher.

D. S. Dharmapalan, Meditation for June 3 in *Upper Room Disciplines 1994.* (Nashville: Upper Room Books, 1993). Used by permission of the publisher.

Stephen V. Doughty, "Glimpsing Glimpses: A Quest for Communal Discernment" in *Weavings*, Vol. X, No. 6, Nov/Dec 1995. (Nashville: The Upper Room, 1995). Used by permission of the author.

Juan G. Feliciano, Meditation for February 12 in *Upper Room Disciplines 1995*. (Nashville: Upper Room Books, 1994). Used by permission of the publisher.

Raymond Fenn, Meditation for May 27 in *Upper Room Disciplines 1995*. (Nashville: Upper Room Books, 1994). Used by permission of the publisher.

Ira Gallaway, Meditation for November 15 in *Upper Room Disciplines 1994*. (Nashville: Upper Room Books, 1993). Used by permission of the publisher.

Loretta Girzaitis, Meditation for July 16 in *Upper Room Disciplines 1992*. (Nashville: Upper Room Books, 1991). Used by permission of the publisher.

Jorge A. Gonzalez, Meditation for January 10 in *Upper Room Disciplines 1995*. (Nashville: Upper Room Books, 1994). Used by permission of the publisher.

James A. Harnish, Meditation for January 25 in *Upper Room Disciplines 1995*. (Nashville: Upper Room Books, 1994). Used by permission of the publisher.

Ron James, Meditation for June 14 in *Upper Room Disciplines 1994*. (Nashville: Upper Room Books, 1993). Used by permission of the publisher.

Linda Johnson, Meditation for April 27 in *Upper Room Disciplines 1995*. (Nashville: Upper Room Books, 1994). Used by permission of the publisher.

K. Cherie Jones, Meditations for March 30, April 2 in *Upper Room Disciplines 1994*. (Nashville: Upper Room Books, 1993). Used by permission of the publisher.

Timothy Kelly: From "A Spirituality of Watch" in *Alive Now*, Nov/Dec 1994. (Nashville: The Upper Room, 1994). Used by permission of the author.

Samuel G. Martinez, Meditation for May 1, 1988 in *The Upper Room Daily Devotional Guide: 1988 General Conference Issue*. (Nashville: The Upper Room, 1988). Used by permission of the author.

Bill Mauldin, Meditation for July 15 in *Upper Room Disciplines 1995*. (Nashville: Upper Room Books, 1994). Used by permission of the publisher.

Ron Mills, Meditation for May 8 in *Upper Room Disciplines 1995*. (Nashville: Upper Room Books, 1994). Used by permission of the publisher.

Frances Mitchell, Meditation for August 6 in *Upper Room Disciplines 1995*. (Nashville: Upper Room Books, 1994). Used by permission of the publisher.

John S. Mogabgab: From "Editor's Introduction" in *Weavings: A Journal of the Christian Spiritual Life*, Vol. X, No. 6, Nov/Dec 1995. (Nashville: The Upper Room, 1995); from "Editor's Introduction" in *Weavings*, Vol. VII, No. 5, Sept/Oct 1992. (Nashville: The Upper Room, 1992); from "Developing the Inner Eye" in *Alive Now*, Nov/Dec 1994. (Nashville: The Upper Room, 1995). Used by permission of the author.

Mary Montgomery, Meditation for November 10 in *Upper Room Disciplines 1995*. (Nashville: Upper Room Books, 1994). Used by permission of the publisher.

Robert Corin Morris, Meditations for March 27, 28 in *Upper Room Disciplines 1995*. (Nashville: Upper Room Books, 1994). Used by permission of the publisher.

Michael J. O'Donnell, Meditation for May 23 in *Upper Room Disciplines 1994*. (Nashville: Upper Room Books, 1993). Used by permission of the publisher.

Phyllis R. Pleasants, Meditation for April 5 in *Upper Room Disciplines 1991*. (Nashville: Upper Room Books, 1990). Used by permission of the author.

Beth A. Richardson, Meditations for August 19, September 1 in *Upper Room Disciplines 1992*. (Nashville: Upper Room Books, 1991). Used by permission of the publisher.

Susan Ruach, Meditation for May 7 in *Upper Room Disciplines 1993*. (Nashville: Upper Room Books, 1992). Used by permission of the publisher.

Betsy Schwarzentraub, Meditations for March 14, 16 in *Upper Room Disciplines 1995*. (Nashville: Upper Room Books, 1994). Used by permission of the publisher.

Robert K. Smyth, Meditation for April 21 in *Upper Room Disciplines 1993*. (Nashville: Upper Room Books, 1992). Used by permission of the publisher.

Barry Stater-West, Meditation for July 23 in *Upper Room Disciplines 1995*. (Nashville: Upper Room Books, 1994). Used by permission of the publisher.

Willie S. Teague, Meditation for September 22 in *Upper Room Disciplines 1995*. (Nashville: Upper Room Books, 1994). Used by permission of the publisher.

Peggy Ann Way, Meditation for September 27 in *Upper Room Disciplines 1995*. (Nashville: Upper Room Books, 1994). Used by permission of the publisher.

Stefanie Weisgram, Meditation for June 21 in *Upper Room Disciplines 1992*. (Nashville: Upper Room Books, 1991. Used by permission of the publisher.

William H. Willimon, Meditations for May 4, 6 in *Upper Room Disciplines 1995*. (Nashville: Upper Room Books, 1994). Used by permission of the publisher.

Janet Wolf, "Shoes and Socks" in *Alive Now*, Mar/Apr 1995. (Nashville: The Upper Room, 1995). Used by permission of the author.

Wendy M. Wright, "Passing Angels: The Art of Spiritual Discernment" in *Weavings*, Vol. X, No. 6, Nov/Dec 1995. (Nashville: The Upper Room, 1995). Used by permission of the author.

Flora S. Wuellner, "Were Not Our Hearts Burning within Us?" in *Weavings*, Vol. X, No. 6, Nov/Dec 1995. (Nashville: The Upper Room, 1995). Used by permission of the author.

Foreword

For more than a decade now, countless people of faith have found a wealth of encouragement for their personal spiritual journeys in two small volumes entitled *A Guide to Prayer for Ministers and Other Servants* and its sequel, *A Guide to Prayer for All God's People.* These books, co-authored by Bishop Rueben P. Job and Norman Shawchuck, have exerted a wide influence in the church ecumenical, proving their appeal to clergy and laity of many denominations. More recently, Rueben Job wrote *A Guide to Retreat for all God's Shepherds,* structured in a manner similar to the Guides to Prayer. Now we are blessed with a new offering written and compiled by Bishop Job. *A Guide to Spiritual Discernment* is a guide to personal and small group prayer specifically focused on discernment. Here is a resource intended for all who struggle to be faithful to God in personal decisions as well as those who have been entrusted with particular decision-making responsibilities in the church.

To those of us who claim the way of Christ as our spiritual heritage, it is a continual challenge to discern the voice of God amid the clamor of competing yet compelling voices. Some of these voices are clearly external: the various and sometimes contradictory messages of family, friends, counselors, doctors, or politicians, for example. Some voices sound plainly from within: the weighing of our thoughts, the searching questions, the voice of conscience and self-honesty. Some voices are internalized from external sources, as is often the case with anxiety, guilt, and self-negating criticism. When uncertain about a future course of action, when faced with difficult choices, when called upon to make decisions in the face of ambiguity, how are we to hear the singular clarity of God's word amid all these voices?

Such a common human predicament forms the context for this book. Throughout the forty days of this exercise, readers will be guided deeper into their questions and opened more fully to new experiences. This time of reflection can be a season of the heart to explore the struggles and graces of spiritual discernment. We follow the path of One who at the culmination of his earthly ministry set his face toward Jerusalem, whose final human agony began in a dark garden struggle to yield his own will to God's, and whose dying act was to commit his spirit into the hands of his unseen and, at that point, impalpable Father. When we choose to seek God's way rather than our own best judgment, we join our Lord in facing toward Jerusalem. We, too, know well the struggle involved in surrendering our will to God, although the outcome of our effort is frequently less faithful than Jesus' example. And often enough we are called to choose and to act even when the clarifying will and comforting presence of God eludes us. Discernment is truly a discipline, in whatever season of life we may practice it.

Readers will find here a simple, classic structure for daily prayer that is balanced and flexible. Scripture readings are thoughtfully chosen and well amplified by selected readings from a variety of authors on spiritual discernment. We can be especially grateful that to set the context for each week's spiritual readings Rueben Job has chosen to offer us the depth and wisdom of his own reflections, culled from years of experience and fidelity to the practice of spiritual discernment. His prayers are likewise a small treasury of direct and heart-felt simplicity.

It is only natural that the more you bring of yourself to these prayers, passages, and reflection opportunities, the more you will find in them. As you open your heart freely to the work of grace through these exercises, God will surely engage you more fully in the art of listening to your life situation and discerning within it the divine intention. God's will always leads to the fullness of life and to spiritual freedom. Discernment is thus a discipline that carries us through the obscurities of confusion and uncertainty to the vivid clarities of Easter promise. May this joyful journey be yours!

— Marjorie J. Thompson
Epiphany, 1996

Introduction

Discerning God's Vision:
Forty Days of Preparation and Reflection

The time frame of forty days has special significance for Christians. We remember Moses and the children of Israel wandering in the wilderness for forty years in search of the promised land. We are especially aware of the forty days Jesus spent in the wilderness facing the subtle and yet hard decision of life. And we annually complete the forty-day Lenten journey from Ash Wednesday to Easter and then from Easter to Pentecost. Exodus and Promised Land are a part of the reality of the church year and of each of our lives.

Thus it is fitting that as Christians seeking to know and do God's will we spend forty days in watching, listening, and reflecting as we seek to discern God's way for us. Our relationship with Jesus Christ can grow stronger and our responsibility to Jesus Christ can grow clearer as we practice methods of discernment as old as Christianity. We will also discover that our relationship to one another is strengthened as together we seek God's will above all else. Congregations often discover a new unity, faith, vitality, mission, and sense of God's nearness as they fervently seek God's will.

The exodus we are called to make is to leave the land of self-centered and self-serving living and decision-making for the promised land of seeking, finding, and doing God's will in all things. To enter the promised land of living in the center of God's will we must leave behind the sin that so easily captures and controls us; that is the desire for our will to be done. Instead we are invited to reach out for the "upward call of God in Christ Jesus" (Phil. 3:14). This requires a radical renunciation of sin and a radical declaration of faith in the God for whom all things are possible. For when our faith in this God without limits is strong, we begin to recognize that our way may not be the best way and God's way is always the best way.

We as the children of Israel have embarked on a journey toward the promised land of God's will in the affairs of our lives and within our congregation. Our faith is not in our prayers, our process of discernment, or a forty-day time frame. Our faith is in the living God who comes to guide and companion those who seek to walk in God's way. While there may be many ways to the promised land of God's full and complete reign, and we as individuals and as a congregation may face many options, we can be sure that there is one most desirable way for us to follow. What is it? Which way is God calling us to go? What is the right decision for us to make? How will we decide the important questions before us? How will we face the temptations of the wilderness and remain faithful and true? With God's help we can be led to discover answers to these and other questions that confront us as we move toward decision making as an individual or as a community of faith.

The people of God are always on the way to the promised land. To be a follower of Jesus is to be a pilgrim, and it is to be on a journey that always leads us toward God and God's goodness. The scriptures remind us that God loves us and seeks to sustain us in all of life. Therefore we can ask for guidance in the confidence that God's way, the very best way, will be made known to us.

The vision of the promised land comes from God. The direction and strength to get there also come from God. But if we are to see the vision and to make the journey, we must be willing to give up what we have for that which is not yet fully realized. We need a willingness and openness to discern, to see God's way and, finally, a yearning to be led in that way alone.

"If you love me, you will keep my commandments. And I will pray the Father, and he will give you another Counselor, to be with you for ever, even the Spirit of truth, whom the world cannot receive, because it neither sees him nor knows him; you know him, for he dwells with you and will be in you" (John 14:15-17, RSV).

— Bishop Rueben P. Job

A Guide *to* Using This Resource

This resource is designed to give an individual, a small group, or a congregation a useful tool to assist in the process of discernment. All persons of faith want to know and do God's will. Yet, in our busy and noisy world it is often hard to hear God's voice. While we all walk by faith, we desire to have some special means of listening to God. Perhaps the greatest work any person of faith is called to is to learn to pay attention to God. To learn how to see God at work in the everyday events of life and to hear God's voice in the sacred scriptures and the life of another is of enormous significance to the person who seeks to live a life of faithfulness. This simple resource is designed to help us in this work of faith.

The resource is designed to be used every day as a way of listening and preparation for the decision making that will come near the end of this forty-day period. The resource includes a structure for daily prayers, a liturgy for covenant groups in which you may gather for discernment and support, and an anthology of readings for each week. In each case you will need a Bible and your hymnal to make the most of this resource. Since busyness is one of our most persistent problems, it will be important for you to determine time and place for this forty-day experience. Set aside some time every day to listen to God's voice, to ask for God's guidance, and to offer your life to God in fidelity and faithfulness.

Each of the liturgies in this guide offers suggested scripture readings and hymns to be sung or read. You may wish to select additional or other hymns or scripture passages for your time of prayer and praise. Feel free to adapt this resource to your individual or corporate needs. Listed below are some brief suggestions and comments about the liturgy for Daily Prayer and Praise.

Prayer of Invitation

Begin this time of prayer and praise by giving full attention to God and by inviting God into your life anew. Use the prayer daily as one way in which you become present to God and invite God to be present to you.

Hymn of Praise
Sing or read the hymn every day. Next to the Bible our hymnbooks are our most helpful resource in listening to and hearing God speak.

Scripture Reading
Read the scripture at least once and always listen for what God is saying to you during the reading.

Reflection and Response
Keep a time of silence to permit the scripture to be God's message for you and for your life for this day. Ask frequently, "What is God saying to me through this passage? What response is being called for from me?" Use a journal to record your insights and questions.

Sacred Reading
Utilize one or more of the readings in this resource or use your hymnbook for some other source for spiritual reading.

Reflection and Response
Once again seek to listen to the material as a letter from God to you seeking to give guidance to your process of discernment. Record your findings for later reference. Writing down our insights and questions often brings clarity to our thought.

Prayer
Each week there are suggestions for our prayers of gratitude and our prayers of petition or intercession. Again, you will want to make this list more specific and add to the list those special areas of thanksgiving and petition that you bring to this time of prayer.

The Lord's Prayer
To pray this prayer is to remember that we are not alone. When we come into the presence of God, we come into the presence of God's people. This prayer that Jesus taught us saves us from simply praying selfish prayers, gives us a glimpse of a

reality larger than our own concerns, and binds us once more to God's vision for all creation.

Closing Prayer of Consecration

In this prayer we declare our willingness to be led by God throughout the activities of the day. It is a time of surrender on the one hand and of picking up our directions and promised sustenance for the day on the other.

Many are praying with you and for you as you prepare to be an instrument in God's hand in the deliberation and decision making of your congregation. If you are using this resource as a guide to personal decision making, ask others to join in prayer with you. May God's grace and peace be yours in abundance as you seek to know and do God's will.

A Guide
for
Daily Prayer

Week 1: Discernment

I. **Prayer of Invitation**
Almighty God, you who have made yourself known to all humankind and to us in times past, make yourself and your way known to us in this time of prayer and reflection. In the name and spirit of Christ. Amen.

II. **Hymn of Praise:** "God, Who Stretched the Spangled Heavens" (*The United Methodist Hymnal*, No. 150)

III. **Scripture Reading**
Sunday	Luke 13:31-35
Monday	1 John 4:1-6
Tuesday	1 John 4:7-12
Wednesday	1 John 4:13-21
Thursday	John 8:12-20
Friday	Deuteronomy 30:11-20
Saturday	Romans 6:1-11, 15-19

IV. **Reflection and Response**

V. **Sacred Reading**

VI. **Reflection and Response**

VII. **Prayer**
Thanksgiving for God's sustaining grace and goodness. Petitions for the following:
Peace in the world, especially . . .
All the churches of God, especially . . .
Our pastors and congregational leaders, especially . . .
All who suffer and are oppressed, especially . . .
All who are prisoners of addiction, especially . . .
All who seek to walk in faithfulness, justice, and righteousness, especially . . .
My own life and witness and for those in my care, especially . . .

VIII. **The Lord's Prayer**

IX.   **Closing Prayer of Consecration**
Loving Creator, we place our lives into your hands with confidence in your love and fidelity. We know that you will lead us into your will and so we ask in confidence, do with us what you will and lead us this day in truth and righteousness. We offer our prayers and our lives in the name of Jesus. Amen.

Readings for Reflection

✝ A Listening Community

Christians at their best are good listeners, and the Christian church, when most faithful, is a listening community. To live with God in this world that God loves requires some intense and intentional listening. So many competing voices are calling for our attention that without concentrated effort and determination we may easily miss what God is saying to us. We may even miss the way and will into which God is trying to lead us.

I wear two hearing aids, and even with them discover that I often mistake one word or phrase for another and often answer questions never asked and take directions never given! Sometimes, even when I remember to listen carefully, have both hearing aids on, and take my time, I still need to ask someone for clarity on the message that I am trying to understand. We all need help to hear clearly and completely the truth of God for our lives and for our world. The Christian community is one of those helps or aids to our hearing clearly the voice and direction of God. The events of the world around us, the events of our lives, the natural world, the scriptures, prayer, worship, sacred reading, a spiritual guide or friend, all can help us to hear.

Faithful guides who have gone before us have suggested that there are several prerequisites to hearing clearly the voice and direction of God. First of all is faith in a God who communicates with us. Our willingness and our effort to listen will be conditioned by our faith in a God who speaks and gives guidance. The wise and faithful leaders of the past also believed that we listen for and to God's voice and direction only when we are intensely dissatisfied with things as they are. It is unlikely that we will hear God's voice calling us to risk, to move out in new mission or with new vision, if we are very comfortable and settled with things the way they are. And perhaps the most important of all is a great love for God and a passion for God's will. When these elements of faith in God, desire for God's way (dissatisfaction with our way), and great love for God and God's will are present in a solitary life or a community, the possibility of one hearing God's voice of guidance is greatly multiplied.

I used to believe that everyone mumbled. My family, my friends, telephone callers, even radio personalities seemed to have lost the ability to speak clearly. Then I was fitted with hearing aids. What a surprise! Everyone spoke with clarity. What had changed? I had accepted help in hearing. Trying to listen and hear clearly the voice of God is not an easy task nor a casual undertaking. Ask God to guide you today and always to the help you need so that you may hear clearly even the slightest whisper of the One who spoke you into being.

—Rueben P. Job

✝ Read Colossians 1:9-12.

His plate was empty. His mouth was full. He was three years old and did not know the word for what he was eating. So he blurted out, "Give me some more of what I've got in my mouth!" This was a little boy who knew when something was good.

I believe that the Colossians knew that they were onto a good thing. From time to time, they probably prayed for more of what they had received. But just in case they had not asked lately, the writer of Colossians intercedes for them: "We have not ceased praying for you." The first prayer is for eyes to see the light, that is, for discernment: "that you may be filled with the knowledge of God's will in all spiritual wisdom and understanding." From this kind of discernment come lives filled with the fruit of good works. The second prayer is for strength: "May you be made strong with all the strength that comes from his glorious power." It is this kind of strength that brings patience and endurance.

What better gifts could be ours as we continue along on our journey of faith than to have the discernment to see God's will and to have some of God's "glorious power" in following the pathway? With these gifts we are able to walk in the same light the saints before us walked in. And what better could we seek each day than to grow more into the likeness of Christ? To have these gifts is truly to have more of what we already have in our mouths!

—Bill Mauldin

✝ What is of God's new reality and what is of the old, dying reality? As we seek conscious and living communion with God, how do we distinguish between God's activity and the many less than benign forces in the world? "He brought me out into a broad place; he delivered me, because he delighted in me" (2 Sam. 22:20). These words, voiced by David celebrating God's help in victory over enemies, offer dramatic images for understanding the mysterious work of discerning the spirits.

On a wilderness sojourn in the deserts of the southwestern United States, David Douglas missed the entrance to a canyon he hoped to explore. Retracing his steps, he noticed a thin crack in the sandstone. Only by shifting his position and altering his perspective did he perceive that this was indeed the canyon entrance, a canyon so narrow and sinuous that at points he could see no more than a few feet ahead.[1] In the course of discerning the spirits, we may pass by openings to fuller life, failing to see them for what they are. At times, our discernment leads us into tight places where decisions must be made even if we can see little of what lies before us. Thus, completing a discernment process has about it an invigorating air of deliverance. From the narrowing of attention and the constraint of necessity imposed on us in a situation of choice, we emerge into a "broad place." We are delivered from the confines of uncertainty by the God who all along has been leading us into the fullness of truth (John 16:13).

True discernment calls us beyond the well-tended gardens of conventional religious wisdom to the margin between the known and the unknown, the domesticated and the wild. We incur risk any time we place ourselves in the presence of that which exists beyond our control. "Without the confidence of faith," comments St. Isaac of Nineveh, "no one will rashly let his [or her] soul go into the midst of terrible and difficult things."[2] How crucial, then, that our efforts to sift and sort the forces shaping our spiritual life be undertaken with some bedrock assurances. King David provides one which cannot be surpassed. We are guided through narrow paths and led to spacious vistas

---

[1] David Douglas, *Wilderness Sojourn: Notes in the Desert Silence* (San Francisco: Harper & Row, 1987), pp. 62-64.

[2] St. Isaac of Nineveh, *On Ascetical Life*, trans. by Mary Hansburg (Crestwood, N.Y.: St. Vladimir's Seminary Press, 1989), Discourse V, no. 49, p. 87.

because God delights in us. Deep in the layers of history, beneath the great upheavals of infidelity that reshape the landscape of our life with God, there abides a divine pleasure in the human creature. In the fullness of time this delight overflowed the bounds of worldly prudence and swept God into our very midst, one with us in suffering and hope. It is always in the gladsome company of this God that our discernment occurs.

—John. S. Mogabgab

✝ Read Psalm 62:5-8.

Most, if not all of us have had our seasons of despair, tribulation, and loneliness. For many of us, dear companions in our journey of faith have provided comfort and support; and to a large extent, serenity has filled us. Thanks be to God for those souls! However, there is a depth in the human spirit that only God can reach. The psalmist recognizes in God the ultimate source of hope as he exclaims, "For God alone my soul waits in silence."

Rock, fortress, salvation, refuge are descriptive words used in reference to God throughout the psalms. Many of our hymns include these words in the texts as reminders of God's strength and closeness in times of trouble.

The psalmist also declares that "on God rests my deliverance and my honor." I like the inclusion of the phrase *my honor*. It tells me that God is concerned for my personal integrity as a human being as well as for my deliverance from trouble.

Recently, I attended the quadrennial organizational meeting of my denomination's General Commission on Christian Unity and Interreligious Concerns in San Francisco. I cherish the corporate worship experiences in the mornings and evenings. One of these—a service of anointing—stands out in my mind. As members of the group anointed each other and imparted mutual blessings, we sang a hymn with the wonderful message of peace and assurance that God alone suffices when we are dismayed. Its haunting melody in a minor key and the serenity of the lyrics filled my soul and reaffirmed to me that all is well as long as I have God.

Calmly and gently we are urged to put our trust in God at all times. *Solo Dios basta*—God is enough.

—José P. Bové

✝ What is the vision that can bring our eyes into focus? What viewpoint has the power to organize and unify our lives? Only one: the will of God. Only as we seek to see all things from the viewpoint of God's will can we find a unity of vision that transcends all personal and worldly interests. In his "edifying address," *Purity of Heart Is to Will One Thing*, Søren Kierkegaard speaks of what I call multiple viewpoints as "double-mindedness," taking the phrase from the last part of James 4:8: "Purify your hearts, you double-minded." This means, says Kierkegaard, "Let your heart in truth will only one thing, for therein is the heart's purity."[3] Furthermore, "If it is certain that a man in truth wills one thing, then he wills the Good, for this alone can be willed in this manner."[4] Though he greatly prefers to speak of willing the Good, it is clear that for Kierkegaard the term is interchangeable with drawing nigh to God or seeking first the kingdom of God. It is looking at all things from the viewpoint of God's will for us and for our world.

The temptation is to let such a vision be not *the* vision, not our "single eye," but rather our primary viewpoint while we still cling to others. Much of Kierkegaard's book is dedicated to examining such subtle and "religious" forms of double-vision. Even with one eye on the Good, our other eye is roving. It may be scanning the crowd to see if they are properly admiring our saintliness. It may be looking ahead to rewards, earthly or heavenly, for being good. It may be looking out for punishment should we fail to be good enough. It may be winking at the secret places in our hearts we wish to keep to ourselves, what Kierkegaard calls willing the Good "up to a certain degree."[5] Until we learn to see through these "evasions," our hearts will never be pure; we will never have a single eye.

—Keith Beasley-Topliffe

✝ Read John 19:38-42; Psalm 31:1-4.

Four days after we graduated from high school, one of my closest friends was killed in a car wreck. Her death was a horrible shock for my friends and me. In the weeks following Heather's death, I wrestled with trying to understand the meaning of life

---

[3] Søren Kierkegaard, *Purity of Heart Is to Will One Thing*, trans. Douglas V. Steere (New York: Harper & Row, 1956), p. 55.

[4] Kierkegaard, *Purity of Heart*, p. 55.

[5] Kierkegaard, *Purity of Heart*, p. 104.

and death. And my Christian faith, nurtured throughout my life by family and churches, came under question as well. Where was God when the man ran the red light and sideswiped her car? Midway through the summer, I decided to trust God with Heather, with my life, and with my grief—a point of conversion for me. The next day my grandfather died, and the task of grieving took a new turn.

That summer of death and grief was a turning point for me. My faith put down deeper roots and became more personal than it had been. I began the disciplines of daily prayer and study and became more active in my church. The crucible of that summer gave me the opportunity to make choices about my response to God.

For Joseph of Arimathea and Nicodemus, Jesus' death was an opportunity to make choices about their discipleship. Up to that point, both had been fairly secret about their faith. Both had prestigious positions that might have been jeopardized by their relationship to Jesus. Yet his death was a catalyst that forced them to reevaluate their loyalty to him. Without their intervention, his body would have been consigned to a common grave. When faced with the choice of remaining secret disciples or being identified as followers of Christ, they chose to go public with their loyalty.

Times of crisis can help us reevaluate our loyalties and respond to God's invitation to a deeper relationship.

—K. Cherie Jones

✝ Grant me, O Lord, to know what I ought to know, to love what I ought to love, to praise what delights you most, to value what is precious in your sight, to hate what is offensive to you.

Do not allow me to judge according to the sight of my eyes, nor to pass sentence according to the hearing of my ears; but to discern with a true judgment between things visible and spiritual, and above all things, always to inquire what is the good pleasure of your will.

—Thomas à Kempis

✝ "Give me somewhere to stand, and I will move the earth." These words of Archimedes, the great mathematician of ancient Greece, summarize a theme that occupied Dietrich Bonhoeffer throughout his active life as a theologian. In the late 1920s, Bonhoeffer found in the myth of the giant Antaeus, who was invincible as long as his feet remained firmly planted on the earth, an image of the Christian who does not turn away from the distress of the world but instead enters fully into it.[6] During the 1930s, when the National Socialists were brutally demolishing the foundations of German life, Bonhoeffer's recurring question was, What is the ground under our feet? And in 1943, while confined in a Berlin prison, Bonhoeffer began to write a play in which the character Heinrich gives voice to the experience of Bonhoeffer's generation: "If one wants to live, there must be ground under one's feet—and we don't have this ground. Therefore we are blown about, hither and yon, by the storm."[7]

Bonhoeffer's search for a spiritual Archimedean point can help us detect the holy ground in our lives. Holy ground is the stable place of clarity and confidence in a turbulent human landscape of shifting values, crumbling hopes, frayed trusts, uncertain commitments. Holy ground is the place of life-giving rootedness in something larger than our own lives, something deep enough and enduring enough to keep us anchored and oriented in the storm. Holy ground is the place at once attractive and fearsome, where God speaks and we listen, the place of empowerment, transformation, and sending forth to live victoriously in a world too often disfigured by the defeat of justice, peace, and human dignity, the place where the gracious rule of God is known and the new creation becomes visible, the place where faith can move mountains (Matt. 17:20). "Give me somewhere to stand, and I will move the earth."

Bonhoeffer found that the ground under our feet, the place from which faith flows forth in redemptive action, is God's unequivocal Yes to all of creation, a Yes uttered in the life, death, and resurrection of Jesus.

—John S. Mogabgab

✝ Some years ago a friend decided to take photography lessons. After several inquiries, she learned of a highly regarded teacher who was about to start a new class. Without hesitation, she signed up.

---

[6] Dietrich Bonhoeffer, *No Rusty Swords*, ed. and introduced by Edwin H. Robertson (London: William Collins Sons & Co., 1965), p. 43.

[7] Dietrich Bonhoeffer, *Fiction from Prison: Gathering Up the Past*, ed. Renate and Eberhard Bethge with Clifford Green, trans. Ursula Hoffmann (Philadelphia: Fortress Press, 1981), p. 46.

Having been a photography buff in high school, I could appreciate all the technical information and professional techniques my friend would undoubtedly be learning from this successful photographer. One day toward the conclusion of the course, I asked my friend what special tricks she had learned about lighting, filters, and printing. Much to my surprise, she replied that she had learned nothing about such things. Indeed, her teacher had spent no time on technical subjects. She went on to explain that, for her teacher, techniques were of secondary importance. The most important thing, the thing on which he had spent the entire course, was teaching his students to develop an eye for the picture. It was his conviction that unless they learned to develop this "eye," no level of technical sophistication would make them good photographers.

In a time of growing interest in spirituality, perhaps applying this teacher's wisdom to the life of faith is just the corrective we need to balance preoccupations with methods of prayer, styles of spiritual direction, techniques for retreat design and leadership. Developing the inner eye of faith involves consciously cultivating a certain joyous expectancy, poised on the rim of hope, regarding God's presence and work in the world. It includes watching for signs of what Evelyn Underhill calls the "unsuspected deeps and great spiritual forces which condition and control our small lives." It means remaining alert for intimations of God's grandeur in the events and people around us. Developing an eye for the "picture" calls us daily to accept the invitation offered by a gracious, surprising God: "I am about to do a new thing; now it springs forth, do you not perceive it?" (Isaiah 43:19).

—John S. Mogabgab

✝ "I will arise before the dawn. . . ."
I will come to precede words and works.

I come, Lord, to precede the awakening of my village,
and all that will be done today
in our houses and our fields.

Before the cock crows, before the Evil One comes,
may You be in this place. Let this day be offered
   to You,
returned to Your right hand!

I come to call You to look upon and bless us all.
No noise yet, no word, no act: among us, Lord,
may You be always first named, first sought, first
    served.
Amen.

—Michel Bouttier

✝ O Jesus, wisdom of God, grant me wisdom that I may always think, speak, and do that which is good in thy sight; save me from evil thoughts, words, and deeds. Have mercy upon thy creatures and upon me, a manifold sinner, that together with all the church I may do what is just for all thy creatures. Amen.

—A prayer of St. Nerses Schnorhali (the gracious one).
Traditionally used to open meetings.

✝ Direct us, O Lord, in all our doings with thy most gracious favor, and further us with thy continual help; that in all our works begun, continued, and ended in thee, we may glorify thy holy name, and finally by thy mercy, obtain everlasting life; through Jesus Christ our Lord. Amen.

—*The Book of Common Prayer*

✝ Read John 6:24-35

David longed for reconciliation with God. From reading David's other psalms, we know he received at least some sense of forgiveness. I wonder, though, if the deepest restoration was unavailable to humanity until God came to us in Christ.

Jesus knew that we are afflicted with an ancient wound. As he taught, he recognized the eternal hunger within us. We hear Jesus offering to satisfy that spiritual hunger. Twice he used the words, "I tell you the truth" (vv. 26, 32, NIV). Each time he was speaking the truth in love as he unmasked misperceptions and redirected understanding. The people sought him after the miracle of the loaves and fishes in order to get more bread. They longed for literal manna like that given to Moses, but Jesus offered a more lasting spiritual food. Jesus offered the bread that was himself.

Again, we are faced with mystery. In the midst of our hunger to get what we need to live in the world, Jesus offers something that seemingly does us little good in the short run. "I am the bread of life. Whoever comes to me will never be thirsty" (v. 35). To receive this soul-sustaining bread, we are simply to "believe in him whom [God] has sent" (v. 29). There for the taking is Jesus himself, the bread of heaven.

Jesus tells us the truth. We work hard for the rewards of the world and always come up hungry. We try to interpret our religion to suit our lifestyle; we would like to keep genuine transformation at bay. But Jesus offers us a greater gift. He exposes our longings and assures us that he has what we most deeply want.

—Gerrit S. Dawson

✝ O God, by whom the meek are guided in judgment, and light riseth up in darkness for the godly: Grant us, in all our doubts and uncertainties, the grace to ask what thou wouldest have us to do, that the Spirit of wisdom may save us from all false choices, and that in thy light we may see light, and in thy straight path may not stumble; through Jesus Christ our Lord. Amen.

—*The Book of Common Prayer*

✝ Read Luke 9:28-32.

It was undoubtedly both mystifying and uplifting for Peter, John, and James to see Jesus transfigured. They had probably not expected anything extraordinary to happen when they accompanied Jesus to the mountain to pray. Perhaps they had hoped to dissuade him from traveling later to Jerusalem, for the disciples were afraid of what would occur there. They were afraid of losing Jesus, and they may have anticipated a quiet time alone with him on the mountain. They were unprepared for what happened as he began to pray.

As Jesus was praying alone, the disciples were shocked into attentiveness. His glory was revealed to them in a wholly unexpected, unforgettable manifestation. "His face changed its appearance, and his clothes became dazzling white" (TEV). The disciples could not understand all that it meant at the time, but they knew the change in Jesus was an important sign from God. They came away from their mountain episode chastened and thoughtful, once more aware that Jesus was no ordinary man.

Jesus' transfiguration was meant to be for the disciples a guidepost, an emphasis, a reminder. Because God's will for us is seldom clear, like the disciples we also need to watch and listen for signs. We need to be attentive to God's will and attentive to the ways open to us to serve—ways to heal the sick, feed the hungry, comfort the lonely, shelter the homeless. We must find opportunities to help transform the world with love.

—Judith Freeman Clark

✝ Guide me, O thou great Jehovah, pilgrim through this barren land.
I am weak, but thou art mighty; hold me with thy powerful hand.
Bread of heaven, bread of heaven, feed me til I want no more;
Feed me til I want no more.

—William Williams (1745)

Week 2: A Broken World

I. **Prayer of Invitation**
Tender shepherd, make your way and your self known to me in this time of prayer and praise. Bring healing to the brokenness in my life and help me to be an answer to another's prayer for healing, mending, and reconciliation. In the spirit of Jesus. Amen.

II. **Hymn of Praise:** "Creating God, Your Fingers Trace" (*UMH*, No. 109)

III. **Scripture Reading**
Sunday   John 11:1-16
Monday   Matthew 4:1-11
Tuesday   Matthew 5:1-12
Wednesday   Mark 10:46-52
Thursday   Matthew 23:13-24
Friday   Galatians 5:13-24
Saturday   Mark 4:35-41

IV. **Reflection and Response**

V. **Sacred Reading**

VI. **Reflection and Response**

VII. **Prayer**
Thanksgiving for God's loving kindness and petitions for:
Those who suffer: the addicted, homeless, poor, hungry, imprisoned, sick, despairing, sorrowing, and dying.
Those who work with the suffering: social workers, doctors, nurses, counselors, chaplains, pastors, and volunteer workers.
The broken places in our community.
Faithful congregations and individuals who reach out to bring healing and hope to the brokenness of our world;
My own life and witness as a follower of Jesus.

VIII. **The Lord's Prayer**

IX.   **Closing Prayer of Consecration**
Crucified One, we bind our lives once more to you with all of the faith and commitment we have to offer. We ask you to hold us close to yourself throughout this day and to lead us in faithfulness all day long. Show us your will and help us to walk in it. We offer our prayers and our lives in the name of Jesus. Amen.

Readings for Reflection

✝ Discernment in a Broken World

We live in a broken world. Even a casual survey of last week's headlines is enough to convince us of the fractured nature of our human family. The pain that many of our sisters and brothers bear seems almost unbearable. We want to reach out and help, but the need is so enormous that we find it easier to shut out the cries for help that come from every point of the compass, lest we ourselves be overcome with the burden of it all.

We need not look to the other side of the world or country or even the other side of our town to find signs of brokenness. Careful self-examination reveals the fractures deep in our own lives. These wounds, old and new, also cry out for healing.

The cries of the broken world are all around us and within us. How can these cries be heard as the voice of God? How can the world's brokenness be a sign of God's vision for a new heaven and a new earth?

Those who have gone before us along the pathway of discernment, seeking only God's will and way, remind us that dissatisfaction with things as they are is one essential element in discovering God's will. When we are settled and very comfortable, it is hard to listen for and respond to God's voice calling us to move out, over, up, beyond, or even to new ministry where we are.

The pain of our world is almost beyond our ability to bear. Because it is, we find ourselves more willing to face the possibility for radical and rapid change of things the way they are for things as they can be when God's reign is fully come. Dissatisfaction with things as they are is one of the ways that we invite the coming of God's reign in our midst.

A second characteristic of those who are able to discern God's will is a passion for God's will. Along with dissatisfaction with things as they are is the yearning for what can be. The vision of the reign of God is not yet complete. The vision is not altogether clear, but we believe that the One who is the truth and who promised to give us the truth will make God's vision known to each of us and to all of us together as we seek to listen and then respond in faithfulness. As followers of Jesus Christ we are all pilgrims on a journey toward God. To turn away from seeking this shared vision is to turn away from Christ.

Another quality of the person or community that is able to hear God's voice and to see God's vision is the capacity to remain open to God. To read the scriptures, to listen to the cries of the world, including our own hearts, to immerse ourselves in prayer, and to act quickly when we sense God calling us to some simple or profound witness or service. Discerning God's vision for a denomination, congregation, family, or solitary life is not a simple or easy endeavor. The One who promised never to leave us also promises to assist us, and therein is our hope.

—Rueben P. Job

✝ I feel very strongly that Christians should be committed to the ancient prophetic vision of human unity. We all belong to one another and that's the way God made us. Christ died to keep us that way. Our sin is that we put asunder what God has joined together. Human unity is not something we are called on to create, only to recognize and then make manifest.

Commitment to human unity has become an urgent pragmatic necessity today. The world has to be managed as a whole and not just as a set of parts.

—William Sloane Coffin

✝ Read 1 Corinthians 12:12-26.

Christ came to break down all the barriers, barriers of race and of color, barriers of free and of unfree. Christ came to end all those labels by which we separate, discriminate, and make judgments. We live in a critical age, and we are encouraged by our society that values individualism and competition to put people on the scales to decide if they are unworthy or if they are of greater or less importance. The criterion is nearly always the extent to which they are useful or not.

And now here is a world turned upside down. Those perceived as the lower, the less interesting, the less honorable—all of these, we are told, are to be respected. They have their role to play. Each one is called and chosen, a unique son or daughter of a loving Father, who accepts each without any sort of qualification and with unconditional love, which does not sort people out and label them as superior or inferior.

We are coming more and more to see that what the Apostle Paul is telling us here is age-old wisdom. The idea of inter-dependence, of the unity, bonding of the parts and the whole, of the relationship through which the individual elements contribute to the harmonious working of the whole is as old as creation itself.

As we deny or hide away the parts of ourselves and the parts of our society which distress us (for example, the aging, those with handicapping conditions, those with a mental illness), we are forgetting the gospel teaching of the Sermon on the Mount, that Jesus speaks with love and reverence of those whom society deems the least—the broken, the small, the damaged. These people are given to us to be part of the whole, and nothing or nobody is to be despised.

—Esther de Waal

☦ If we look at the scriptures, if we look at the life of Christ, we become aware of many models of faith formation that the scriptures give to us.

One of the models in scripture that is very important is the model of watching. Toward the end of the Gospel of Matthew, a number of passages refer quite directly to watching and waiting. In chapter 24, Jesus says, "Keep awake therefore, for you do not know on what day your Lord is coming" (24:42). And in verse 44, "Therefore, you too must stand ready because the Son of man is coming at an hour you do not expect" (JB). Then in chapter 25 we have the parable of the ten bridesmaids, some with the oil, some without the oil; but the final statement is this: "So stay awake, because you do not know either the day or the hour" (25:13, JB). In all of these passages there is a waiting and watching for what is to come.

Watching and waiting have been observed by the church from the most ancient times down to the present.

The purpose of vigil, the purpose of watching, is to bring us to reconciliation with God and with all creation, allowing us to be ready for the coming of Christ. Daily contact with the word of God guides us in keeping watch. With openness of heart, with obedience to the deepest call of God in our spirit, we listen to what God is saying to us, through others and through the church, about how to be born and brought back to the fullness of the image of God.

—Timothy Kelly

✝ Read Acts 11:1-3.

Jewish Christians resisted the first wave of Gentile Christians surging into the early church. Covenant people struggled to interpret this new attitude toward persons with whom they were formerly forbidden to associate. The new folks ate differently, dressed differently, acted differently. Unexpected guests were spoiling Jerusalem's salvation party.

Why do we so often feel threatened by those who do not share the same experiences, traditions, or stories that shape our lives? The awareness that God welcomes those who are "not like us" calls into question what makes us *us*. We grow accustomed to thinking of ourselves, our fellowship, our spiritual journey in a certain way. Newcomers trouble us.

Perhaps our desire for certainty in our relationship with God causes our suspicion toward new arrivals in the church family. The spirit of God, however, dismantles our misbegotten attempts to secure a faith by fencing in ourselves and our faith community. God continually reveals the larger boundaries of grace. The divine spirit perpetually falls on a vast diversity of human lives, even as they approach the borders of life with God within a faith community. To welcome them leads us toward greater understanding of God's will for all humanity.

—Ron Mills

✝ When Jesus faced the temptations in the wilderness, he had just heard himself named as beloved child. What did he have to face in his own heart that kept him from knowing, from really embracing that truth? What groping did he do in the desert to find the level where the Spirit moves free? What attentiveness, what discrimination was called for? Scripture says that when he was done, angels came and ministered to him. They must have done more than touch him as they passed; they must have unfurled their wings and beat the air and sung out for sheer joy.

—Wendy M. Wright

✝ Read Revelation 7:13-14.

I spent time last year on a medical mission team in Honduras, the second most impoverished country in the Western Hemisphere. I think of those whom we met there. Christians in Honduras are working against great odds to alleviate some of the suffering of people. There is not enough food, little medical care, and much pain, but also much good work among the poor.

Why is there so much suffering? Hunger and thirst, brief temporary experiences for me, are the stuff of everyday life for countless millions.

"When I see suffering like this, particularly among the children," said one of our mission team members, "I become angry with God." Why, if God is good, is there such heartache and pain?

The vision given to John in Revelation is not the answer to such an awesome question. Yet it is an answer. When the curtain is lifted in heaven and the end toward which all creation is moving is revealed and the Lamb begins to reign in power and glory, note toward whom the Lamb moves. Not toward the self-satisfied, the well-heeled, and the well-fed. The Lamb declares that those who have been hungry, who had little but tears to drink, shall hunger and thirst no more. No longer offered the false comfort of the broken promises of the rich or the cheap consolations of the superficially pious, now "God will wipe away every tear from their eyes."

Who are these before the throne, these singled out for special care by the Lamb?

—William H. Willimon

✝ Holy Spirit, baptize me today. Let Your fire rekindle the instrument that You have chosen. My outer nature destroys itself day after day. According to Your unforgettable promise, continually renew my inner nature. You know the weakness of my body: languor, apathy, sleep. You see, locked in impotence, these gifts of Your grace in me: these revelations, these approaches, these struggles, and these joys. Why these words that stick in my throat? These babblings? These hesitations? Have You lost Your grip on me? Could I be stronger than You in my body? O, triumph over my heaviness! Let the mass of my flesh not block Your surge; let Your inner coming be translated into deeds and evident signs. Blaze Your trail across my body; cleanse it so it may become a display window; exorcise it so that it will be a bent bow. Yes, Lord, stretch this slack cord till it can finally make Your arrows sing. As a bent bow, so I would like my body to be in Your service! O, Holy Spirit, make of my whole being a new creation!

—Michel Bouttier

✝ Read John 17:20-23.

From early on the church has been split by disunity. Yet, the Gospel puts great emphasis on the inherent unity between God, the Father, and Jesus, the Son. Their unity finds expression through the church. Obviously, we do not accept all the implications that unity has for our life together, or perhaps, more accurately, we pretend to a unity that we do not actually experience.

John's Gospel was written some years after the events described in it, probably toward the end of the first century. The author is concerned with bringing the reader to the point of decision; that is, to belief that Jesus is the son of God and that real life will be experienced through him.

The church's future depends on belief transmitted through the friends of Jesus. Unity among Christians is necessary—not a unity which requires everyone to agree on every doctrine but a unity out of which all work together for one purpose, proclaiming God's kingdom that the world may believe. When the Christian community is divided about its purpose, then its message is always weakened and perhaps meaningless.

John is making the point that witness to the united life of the church is not only a confirmation of God's revelation in Jesus but also a sign that the objective of that revelation is being achieved. The question for each of us in relation to this is: Do we really care about working with others for true unity? If so, are we sufficiently concerned to make it a priority of our witness?

—Raymond Fenn

✝ "Strive to enter through the narrow door; for many, I tell you, will try to enter and will not be able" (Luke 13:24). This scripture and others like it scared me when I was young. In fact, they still leave me with an anxious feeling. How will I know which door is the right door? Which door is narrow enough? What if I can't find it?

There are many confusing signals for today's traveler on the spiritual way. I've seen no signs pointing to the narrow door.

There are many that show me the "true" way, or the most efficient way; the narrow way is not so popular.

I imagine that the narrow door is off the beaten path, that we have to do some searching to find it. We may be alone on the journey much of the time, but there are others who have gone before us and who leave us hints and markers. I wonder what are some of the signs that help us find the "narrow doorness" of life.

Compassion. The world is close to us today with instant news reporting. There are wars and famines and murders in our living rooms. It seems impossible to enter the way of compassion and not be overcome. The way of compassion means not so much generating our own compassion as opening ourselves to be channels of God's infinite compassion.

The unbeaten path. Going along with the crowd seems easier and safer. (Could so many be going the wrong way?) The unbeaten path leads to places of quiet and pain and solitude. It may mean working for peace while the crowd is screaming, "Nuke them!"

Self-examination. Self-examination on the spiritual path means setting ourselves against God's plumb line to see where we need to be shored up or evened out. Entering the narrow door may mean choosing to enter a difficult process of healing old wounds or giving up self-destructive behaviors.

—Beth A. Richardson

✝ My soul is troubled. What shall I say?
Father, deliver me from this hour?
Father, glorify Your name!
You know how heavy crying and pain are for me.
I withdraw prudently from trouble so as not to be rattled.
Grant me, Lord, on the contrary,
    to give myself over to suffering and to tears.
Let me flee from nothing, but come defenseless and
    without armor to receive blows, to endure them
    and, in
Jesus Christ, to bear them to the end.

—Michel Bouttier

✝ Read Colossians 3:1-11.

The Christ of Colossians is the universal Christ, the Christ who is all in all and is able to unify the people of God.

Paul believed that Christ was fully divine. Everything was created through him and for him. We, as believers, are raised with Christ and seek our connectedness to all that Christ is connected to so that we participate in the unity.

Paul declared that in this new world order we all become equal. We become responsible. We become just. We become one. The old social order that divides us, the old ways of behaving that divide us, the sins of idolatry and apostasy are all gone. Peace and justice replace them—not just for ourselves but for the whole universe!

There are those who say that all human life is connected. We are one in our cellular makeup. Some would say that the whole universe is interrelated. The socio-economic world must be one in terms of justice for all. And finally, we are all connected spiritually as the children of the one God. Christ does away with those elements which would divide and separate us in whatever dimension.

How marvelous is our God! Let us sing a song of thankfulness:

Let the shadow on our soul lift.
Let the gloom of our sin be dispelled.
Let the ring of self-awareness break the silence.
Let the fire of repentance blaze hot.
Let the cry of thankfulness bellow out.
Let the ashes of justice fall on the neighbor.
CHRIST IS ALL AND IN ALL.
Amen. Amen. Amen.

—Frances Mitchell

✝ Down in the human heart, crushed by the tempter,
feelings lie buried that grace can restore;
touched by a loving heart, wakened by kindness,
chords that were broken will vibrate once more.
Rescue the perishing, care for the dying,
Jesus is merciful, Jesus will save.

—Fanny J. Crosby, 1869

✝ Someone needs you, Lord, kum ba yah.
Someone needs you, Lord, kum ba yah.

—African-American spiritual

✝ Here I am, Lord,
once more to plead the case of my village before You.
I do not know how to penetrate the opaque veil that
   conceals from us the nearness of Your Kingdom.
I do not know how to tear down the artificial
   decorations
of "religion"; behind them we would find freedom itself,
joy, the glory of Your presence!

O Lord, let me not cease, at least,
   to present my village to You.
In prayer let the fog that hinders each and all of us
   be dissipated—let that be my ministry!

Before You I have free access;
I have this grace to be able to speak to You about us,
   knowing that You hear, that You understand.
Our wretchedness—have You not shared it in Christ?
                                          —Michel Bouttier

✝ Read Jeremiah 29:1, 4-7.
   When you are far from home, lonely, cut off from all that is familiar, it is a tall order to be told that the welfare of the people where you are is as important as your own well-being. The awesome God continues to push at the edges of experience and understanding. For the exiled Israelites, first God did just that with advice to settle in fully, enjoy life where they now were. Now here is a word about seeking the peace and welfare of that place and a clear word that the prosperity of the city where they dwell is inextricably linked with their own prosperity.
   These words seem to erase any sense we have that we can maintain our identity in some sort of splendid isolation from the environs and circumstances that surround us. In fact, deep involvement in the community—be it city or village or in between—is part of what God expects of those who know the Divine Presence. Not only is the promise that we cannot be taken beyond the concern of God, the promise is also that we can find ourselves involved with surprising people we have not known and with them find a common welfare.
   No matter how far beyond the concern of God some places or some people seem to us—irreverent, uninterested in God,

unaware of God in their midst—our well-being is intimately woven into the welfare of the larger society.

—Judith Craig

✝ There is a balm in Gilead to make the wounded whole;
There is a balm in Gilead to heal the sinsick soul.

Sometimes I feel discouraged, and think my work's in vain.
But then the Holy Spirit revives my soul again.
There is a balm in Gilead to make the wounded whole;
There is a balm in Gilead to heal the sinsick soul.

Don't ever feel discouraged, for Jesus is your friend,
And if you look for knowledge he'll ne'er refuse to lend.
There is a balm in Gilead to make the wounded whole;
There is a balm in Gilead to heal the sinsick soul.

If you can't preach like Peter, if you can't pray like Paul,
Just tell the love of Jesus, and say he died for all.
There is a balm in Gilead to make the wounded whole;
There is a balm in Gilead to heal the sinsick soul.

—African-American spiritual based on Jeremiah 8:22

✝ Read 1 Timothy 2:1-7.

Running throughout these verses is an emphasis upon the universality of the gospel and its universal relevance. We are *not* dealing here with the doctrine of universalism (that all humanity will be saved). We are told that God desires for all to be saved and that in Christ Jesus the ransom for all has been paid. The focus is on the universal relevance of the gospel.

Prayers are to be made for *all humanity*. God desires *all humanity* to be saved. Jesus "gave himself as a ransom for *all*." We hear echoes of (1) Paul's claim that God was reconciling the *world* through Christ (2 Cor. 5:18-19); (2) John's famous word that "God so loved the *world* that he gave his only Son" (John 3:16); and (3) Jesus' claim that if he is lifted up he will draw *all* humanity to himself (John 12:32).

If the gospel is for everyone, what effect does that have not only on our prayer life but also on how we live in relationship with others? If the gospel is intended for all, what does that say about how we receive all people into the church and into our lives? If the gospel is for Christians and non-Christians, what claim does that make on the way we relate to non-Christians?

There is no greater call to mission and evangelism than these verses. If all humanity is capable of receiving God and if God wishes all to be saved, then we who know of our salvation must go beyond praying for everyone. Faithful living calls us to love as we have been loved and to have in us the mind of Christ.

—Willie S. Teague

✝ Dona nobis pacem, pacem. Dona nobis pacem.
Give us peace, peace. Give us peace.

—traditional Latin

✝ Read Ephesians 2:11-22.

How can I feel at home in a world that is fragmented, moving in so many directions at the same time, and in which we pass one another uncaringly while all of us are searching for home? Boredom, resentment, and depression issue from a disconnectedness. A feeling of not belonging is a malady of our time. To paraphrase Augustine, our spirits will wander restlessly, longing for home, until they are at home with God.

The second chapter of Ephesians gives us hope in our search for home. No one needs to stand outside, looking longingly or resentfully for peace—for home. "Your world was a world without hope and without God. But now in union with Christ Jesus you who once were far off have been brought near through the shedding of Christ's blood. . . . Thus you are no longer aliens in a foreign land, but . . . members of God's household" (NEB).

We are members of God's household—God's children—at home with our Creator and Sustainer. In the midst of pain, sin, and disillusionment, the gracious invitation comes to dwell with our gentle Guardian. Retired United Methodist bishop Leontine Kelly, preaching at Ocean Grove, New Jersey, said that when she graduated from seminary after much struggle and sacrifice, others may have been walking to "Pomp and Circumstance," but she was marching to "Amazing Grace." Zacchaeus, the penitent thief on the cross, the woman who touched Jesus' garment—all experienced God's grace, that same amazing grace that continues to welcome us home.

—George W. Bashore

Week 3: A Broken Body

I. **Prayer of Invitation**
God of healing and wholeness, I invite your presence into the midst of my own incompleteness. Show clearly the reality of my brokenness and lead me now and always into your way of healing and wholeness. In the name of Jesus. Amen.

II. **Hymn of Praise:** "O God Who Shaped Creation" (*UMH*, No. 443)

III. **Scripture Reading**
Sunday	Matthew 21:1-11
Monday	John 19:1-11
Tuesday	John 19:12-16
Wednesday	John 19:17-27
Thursday	John 19:28-37
Friday	John 19:38-42
Saturday	Matthew 26:69-75

IV. **Reflection and Response**

V. **Sacred Reading**

VI. **Reflection and Response**

VII. **Prayer**
Thanksgiving for God's redeeming and healing presence. Petitions for the following:

For all denominations and especially for the denomination where God has called me to live out my discipleship.

For the congregations, members, pastors, and all volunteer workers;

For boards and agencies, colleges and seminaries, hospitals, care centers, and all ministries that offer the healing love and justice of the risen Savior;

For my congregation and for burning desire to know God's will and for desire and faith to follow God's will alone.

VIII.   **The Lord's Prayer**

IX.   **Closing Prayer of Consecration**
Tender shepherd, we offer to you all that we are, aware of our incompleteness, and ask for your healing presence in our lives and in the life of this congregation and of every congregation. We are ready to take the next step toward completeness. Show us the way. In the name of Jesus Christ. Amen.

Readings for Reflection

✝ Discernment in a Broken Body

The church is not perfect. Sometimes we wish it were. Sometimes we even think it is. There are those moments of Christ in action through the church that move us to joyous thanksgiving. There are also those moments that painfully remind us that the church is made up of persons like ourselves. We are the Body of Christ, the Church. And we are persons who are a mixture of motives, hopes, faith, fears, anxiety, and who have been shaped by family, culture, education, and the church itself. And we carry all of who we are into the church. So it should not be surprising to us that the Body of Christ is broken and fractured. The conflicts, halting discipleship, fragile faith, timid witness, and qualified commitment are a natural outgrowth of who we are as individual Christians.

While we may look at the church in its various expressions with joy at times and dismay at others, we must remember that new life is possible. Transformation can begin today. Resurrection power is available to us and can be invested in the church this very moment. With God's help we can initiate change this very day!

This is true because our first line of defense against further brokenness is within each of us. My efforts to stop the brokenness and to take the first step to reform and transform the church must begin with me. My prayer for a holy Church marked by righteousness and love can be answered only as I yield my life to the way of Jesus Christ and the power of the Holy Spirit. The transformation begins with me. What a liberating thought! I am not powerless and without options. With God's help I can surrender my life to the transforming, life-giving power of the

Holy Spirit and in that very moment begin the journey toward the wholeness and faithfulness I want to see in the Church.

Discernment for the Christian community begins with the individual Christian. Do I want to know God's will more than anything else? This question is the entryway into discernment. And it can be answered with affirmation only by those who love God and have learned to trust God. If we have any higher priority in our search for God's guidance, we will not be able to trust our discernment. I must spend enough time in prayer and faithful listening to the voice of God to be brought to that moment of trust and surrender when I can give up my preconceived ideas and become open to God's idea. My first concern is not my desired result. My first concern is always God and the fidelity of our relationship, and then the result of my discernment efforts will come quite naturally. We know that God is completely faithful, and we must be alert, prayerful, open, and ready to respond in obedience if we are to be led toward greater faithfulness on our part.

Obedience is the next essential step in seeking God's will. The word obedience has a bad reputation in our time but a very positive record in humankind's recorded relationship with God. Those who were ready to follow God's direction received the guidance needed. The biblical record suggests God's desire to lead a faithful people. And yet it seems that God is reluctant to make clear the road to faithfulness to those who are not willing to walk along that road. Many who have gone before us have declared that we cannot know God's will unless we commit our way to that will, even before we ask for clarity on what that will is for us.

Can Christians know God's will? Can the Church know God's will? Can our congregation know God's will? Nearly two thousand years of experience shout a resounding yes! But it will not be easy to know God's will because such knowledge begins with us. We first must offer our lives to God in all of the completeness we can bring and then listen in all the ways we know for the voice of the One who alone can transform our lives, our congregations, our denomination, the entire Body of Christ, and even the world. As we listen, hear, and respond, we will discover transformation occurring within and around us, and perhaps even to our surprise, we will begin to see clearly God's will. May it be so!

—Rueben P. Job

✝ It is told that Bernadette of Lourdes, during the weeks of her visions of the Lady at the grotto, was handed a bottle of holy water by a nervous friend suspicious of the nature of these apparitions. How did they know it was Mary, or even a benignant spirit? Perhaps it was an evil spirit haunting the grotto. Bernadette was told to test the vision by sprinkling the ground with the holy water and to challenge the vision: "Madame, if you are of God, step forward. But if not, leave this place." Bernadette told them afterwards that the Lady smiled and rather playfully moved forward a few paces on the rock.

I loved the story, but I remember thinking when I first read it, "If only it were as easy as that!" Only too often my own ambiguities and mysteries of decision making have resembled a small radio we have in our kitchen. We will tune into a classical music station, but often when we walk across the kitchen, the channel spookily shifts all by itself, almost imperceptibly, to a talk show or rock music station. The channel had been clear and strong in the beginning, but apparently by walking around we had interfered with the radio waves and the "alien" crept in.

What might be the equivalent of holy water when we make a decision, undertake a project, enter into a commitment which seems at first to be a wholesome one but ends up in a muddle and a morass? Looking back, we often see what went wrong. Sometimes we realize that we have indeed tuned into the wrong channel from the beginning due to deception (including our own self-deception) or because we were out of touch with who we really are and what we really want. Or, even sadder, we can see a good, guided beginning eaten away, destroyed by many small corrupting choices along the way. But why was the initial discernment so clouded? Why could we not hear and recognize the voice of the living God in the midst of this ambiguity?

The other day I was rereading that wise, ancient parable of the Garden of Eden. It suddenly struck me that the usually overlooked irony in the story is that the very thing the deceiver promised the humans, discernment (". . . your eyes will be opened . . . knowing good and evil," Gen. 3:5), was precisely the thing withheld! They were shown one thing only, that they were naked and vulnerable, and that was all they could discern. In short, the human being was stuck forever with the terror of choice, but the clear discernment (as scriptures and all of human history make cruelly clear) has been all along generally in a state of "white-out." In his letter focusing on the perplexities and signs of discernment, John warns us with hard, loving realism:

> *Beloved, do not believe every spirit, but test the spirits to see whether they are from God; for many false prophets have gone out into the world. . . . Little children, keep yourselves from idols.*

(1 John 4:1, 5:21)

—Flora S. Wuellner

✝ Read Luke 4:21-30.

What went wrong? Why was Jesus rejected in his hometown?

The answer may be rooted in the prophetic tradition to which Jesus referred (1 Kings 17:8–18:1). Many widows of Israel suffered in the drought, but Elijah helped a foreigner in Sidon. Israel had many lepers, but Elisha healed a Syrian named Naaman (2 Kings 5). By their actions, the prophets shattered the illusion of particularity. They waged a frontal assault on racial, ethnic, and religious provincialism, expressing God's universal love.

Jesus, too, pushed against the conventional boundaries of actions and beliefs. At Nazareth he proclaimed good news to the poor, release to the captives, recovery of sight to the blind, and freedom for the oppressed. His listeners, at first, were pleased by his words. But when the implications reached their souls, they rose in anger to throw Jesus out of town.

I grew up in a homogeneous community, much like Nazareth I suspect. We knew there were people in the world who were different from us, but we suspected they were wrong. One of my first mentors to assault the provincialism of my life was a seminary professor named Gilbert James, who figured that people had not really heard the gospel until it made them angry. When we find the place where Jesus offends us, we have probably found the point at which the gospel can transform our lives.

Listen to your life. Where does Jesus make you angry? Where does the gospel push against the comfortable boundaries of your experience? Where does God's love stretch your acceptance of people who are beyond your normal comfort zone?

—James A. Harnish

✝ Lord, let me today be docile in Your hand
and at the same time spontaneous;
faithful yet constantly on a new way.

Grant me fullness of obedience and fullness of freedom;
total dependence and total independence;
full submission and full release.
Being out front and behind in that,
following You, I will walk before You.

Let everything in me be
   response and responsibility,
      gratitude and initiative,
         imitation and discovery.

Father, let me be Your child!

—Michel Bouttier

✝ Discernment is about discriminating: sifting through and evaluating the evidence of our focused attention. It is not, however, identical to problem solving. It is not simply a question of lining up the pros and cons concerning a particular decision we must make and then judging which choice is feasible or determining which gains the most support or which will benefit us, or others, in the long run.

Discernment is more like the turning of the sunflower to the sun, or the intuitive hunch of the scientist seeking new and creative solutions for unexplainable, contradictory observations, or the restless seeking of a heart longing to find its way home to an estranged lover, or the artistry of the musician, sculptor, or choreographer delineating in sound, stone, or the human body the emergent, self-propellant, rightful line that says "yes."

Discernment is about feeling texture, assessing weight, watching the plumb line, listening for overtones, searching for shards, feeling the quickening, surrendering to love. It is being grasped in the Spirit's arms and led in the rhythms of an unknown dance.

The spiritual heritage of Christianity provides us with a number of theories and techniques of discernment. Ignatian discernment (originated by the sixteenth–century Spaniard, Ignatius of Loyola, founder of the Jesuits) stresses the discrimination of one's affectivity—how one feels. Put simply (although Ignatian discernment both in theory and practice is not simple), one is asked to pay attention to the "consolations" or "desolations" that result as one considers possibilities or undertakes actions. In general, and in the long term, for persons already embarked on a journey of faith, the Spirit of God presents itself as consoling, as peace and goodness. Spirits of other origins tend ultimately to give rise to experiences of confusion, disharmony, and anxiety.

In the seventeenth and eighteenth centuries, The Society of Friends, or Quakers, developed a mode of communal discernment, a listening in shared silence, to the "weight" or groundedness of various alternatives proposed for consideration. The silence of the Quaker meeting itself, in its gravity or depth, was discriminated and the hearing of such depth validated by the intuitive acknowledgment of those gathered.

The writings of a sixteenth–century Carmelite mystic, John of the Cross, provide us with another alternative or complementary interpretation of discernment. A poet and spiritual theologian, John wrote of the desire of the human soul for its beloved, God. He described the process of this intense desiring as a gradual, ecstatic, painful process of stripping away all objects of desire and coming to know that it is only God, in God's unfathomable, unknowable mystery, where desire's end can be found. Desire propels one into intimacy with a love whose truest dynamics are death and resurrection. John often interprets the experience of inner suffering and pain that result from responding to divine desire as a sign that the spiritual purgation or emptying necessary for divine union is taking place.

Such systems of discernment, among others, give to the greater Christian community a variety of means by which to enter the arms of the Spirit and begin the dance.

—Wendy M. Wright

✝ *Joshua did as he was told.*

(Joshua 5:15, TEV)

Joshua sought God's direction throughout his life. This faithfulness prepared him to face the unknown and to make tough decisions with confidence in God's will. It should be no surprise, then, that Joshua's response to the commander of God's army was simply to ask, "What do you want me to do?" and then do it.

But perhaps it was not quite that easy. After all, Joshua was human. I can picture him wondering if he clearly understood what God desired. The instructions God gave him for capturing Jericho must have seemed foolish to a military man. Yet he listened and obeyed.

How I long to be like Joshua—to be more faithful to God's call in my life when I am facing the unknown! I long to be more receptive to God's direction and more joyfully obedient when there is a tough decision to make.

There are times when I hesitate to follow God's leading. Maybe I think the experience will be too painful, or maybe I doubt that I "have what it takes," or maybe I fear the outcome, or . . .

—R. Kay Barger

✝ Read Isaiah 6:1-8.

When we compare ourselves to the power and majesty of God, we pale in comparison. We are overwhelmed by God's power. We are even more easily overwhelmed by the scope of the problems in the world today.

This is the scene that opened before Isaiah. He beheld the glory of the Lord and his own unworthiness in the light of that glory. Isaiah knew his limitations. He knew that he had sinned and fallen short of God's expectations. He felt lost.

And yet he was open to the intervention of the Lord. God used divine power to remove Isaiah's sin from him. Having been cleansed of his "spirit dirt," Isaiah then answered the summons to do the Lord's work.

Too often we want to be relieved of our sins. We want a clean record. But having received that, we fall back into our old ways. God wants us to use our spiritual cleanliness as a beginning point of service. What good is it to be freed from our sins if we fail to let go of them?

Forgiveness is not only freedom from our past; it is also freedom for our future. When we entrust ourselves to God for that future, we will never be disappointed.

—Michael J. O'Donnell

✝ *[Joshua said,] "Now if you are unwilling to serve the LORD, choose this day whom you will serve. . . . as for me and my household, we will serve the LORD."*

(Joshua 24:15)

Living is a matter of making decisions. It seems that a decision making process precedes every human action: what to wear, what to eat, when to drive, where to work. Some decisions have little or no consequences; others have major consequences.

Governments are constantly making decisions for their nations. Institutions, including the church, impact millions of people. Humanity has suffered the effects of wars because of wrong decisions. Humanity's record leaves much to be desired.

God offers us the great choice: to serve God or not to serve God. After making my decision to serve God, all other decisions that I make are based on one basic question: Will it serve God's purpose?

—Samuel G. Martinez

✝ Here I am, Lord: I am the offering of the parish.
With their work, their money, they feed me.
They do what they can so I can be there, to pray
   to You.
My life is their offering to You.
For their sake, accept me.
Forgive me for continually taking
myself back from them and from You:
from them who have called me,
from You who have redeemed me.

Lord, at least in the work of prayer
let me accomplish the task which You
have entrusted to me. Amen.

—Michel Bouttier

✝ Read Psalm 36:5-10.

There are two very different perspectives in the Old Testament. One is exclusive and isolationist and presents the people of Israel as holding a special, privileged place in their relationship with God. Ezra, Nehemiah, and Esther, among others, represent this understanding. The other perspective, represented by books such as Ruth, Jonah, Job, and others, offers a more universal view. For these authors, the doctrine of election speaks not of Israel's privileges but of its responsibilities. The author of Psalm 36 evidently was a representative of this second line of thought.

The psalmist celebrates the magnitude of God's "steadfast love" (Hebrew *hesed*). No ordinary love, this love is one of God's most distinctive features. It is boundless, as deep as the deepest ocean, as high as the highest sky. No creature in the universe is left out of its grasp. This love is addressed not just to Israel: "All people may take refuge in the shadow of your wings."

We in the church claim to be successors and heirs to the promises and blessings given to Israel. Let us therefore remember that we, just as they, are called not to privileges but to responsibilities and that God's steadfast love is extended to all, not just to those of us who are part of the church. Refuge under the divine wings is available to all who seek it. Let us learn to accept as our brothers and sisters all those who seek refuge to God, united under the protection of this divine love which offers us the comfort of an everlasting refuge.

—Jorge Gonzalez

Week 4: God Made Visible

I. **Prayer of Invitation**
God made known in the face of Jesus, come and reveal yourself to me in this time of prayer and reflection. Help me to come before you in openness so that I may receive you more fully into my life and to receive your guidance in all that I do and am. In the name of Jesus Christ. Amen.

II. **Hymn of Praise:** "Christ Is Alive" (*UMH*, No. 318)

III. **Scripture Reading**
Sunday	John 20:1-18
Monday	1 John 4:1-6
Tuesday	1 John 4:7-21
Wednesday	Matthew 25:31-46
Thursday	John 14:8-14
Friday	John 14:15-24
Saturday	Matthew 28:16-20

IV. **Reflection and Response**

V. **Sacred Reading**

VI. **Reflection and Response**

VII. **Prayer**
Thanksgiving for God's presence and guidance in your life and in the Church.
Petitions for:
Leaders and all who join you in seeking only God's will;
All who this day face decisions that must be made;
The suffering and dying;
Those who long for the new life that only God can bring.

VIII. **The Lord's Prayer**

IX. **Closing Prayer of Consecration**

Living and present God, we thank and praise you for your presence with us in all of the experiences of life. We seek your guidance in every decision of life, and even as we ask for your help, we offer our lives to you anew and ask you to do with us what you will. Our promise to you today is to follow wherever you may lead us. We are yours. Amen.

Readings for Reflection

✝ Hearing God's Voice: Seeing God's Way

We do not see God up close, face to face every day. Or do we? Could it be that God is with us at all times, seeking to be our guide and companion as well as our Lord and Savior? Our scripture readings for the week suggest that the answer is yes. We are never outside the care and loving gaze of God, and we can learn how to live more fully in the awareness of and surrender to that presence. To do so is to open ourselves to guidance and direction in all of life.

You have been given responsibility for decision making. It is a large responsibility, and the issues are complex and seldom clearly one way or the other. Even when we have gathered all the facts and looked at and listened to all the evidence, the answer may still be unclear. We bring our best thoughts and all of our previous experiences to the decision making process, and still we find that prejudice, half truths, insufficient evidence, and lack of wisdom leave us uncertain about God's way in the matter.

At times like this we long for the assurance of God's presence with us. We yearn to ask Jesus, who always reflected God's will, what our decision should be, what really is God's will in this matter. We would seek to know how we can discern that our decisions are not our own, not where the popular opinion is, not what is easy or cheap, not even what will please the most persons or defeat someone we don't like. Rather, one might ask, "What is God's will? What does God desire around this concern I have? What decision would I make if I were to block out all other interests and seek to please only God?"

To ask these primary questions is to begin to open ourselves to God's guidance and gradually to lower the volume of all the other competing voices that seek to influence our decision making. It is to place ourselves in a position where we can receive God's guidance in our personal and corporate decision making process.

Competing voices are always around us, and some of them loudly proclaim that they are or have heard the voice of God and consequently we should follow them. How to decide which voice to listen to is an essential step to discerning God's will. In other words, which voice are we to follow? Faithful Christians want to follow the way of and do the will of the God made known through Jesus Christ, the scriptures, our own experiences, and the experiences of those faithful persons who have gone before us. In other words, preparation for decision making began a long time ago, and we can bring the experience of a long–time companionship with God to our decision making.

Added to our experience of walking with Jesus and daily seeking the guidance of the Holy Spirit is our listening to the scriptures for God's voice addressing us in our daily reading and reflection. We can place ourselves under the scriptures, and let them address us rather than placing ourselves over the scriptures, seeking to use them to fortify our own position. Our time of prayer can become a time of listening for an answer to a simple petition of "show me your way." As a matter of fact, those who seek to walk with God in the world are always praying "show me your way" and face every event of their lives with the question, "What is God saying to me though this experience?"

The Gospels and book of Acts give a glimpse of the dependence upon God for guidance that marked every decision the early church was called upon to make. The promise to the individual Christian and to the church has always been that wisdom and guidance were available for the asking to those who sought only God's will. We have nearly two thousand years of testimony declaring that such an earnest request will be heard and answered. Therefore, you may ask for guidance with assurance and respond with confidence as God guides your decision making.

—Rueben P. Job

✝ Read Isaiah 55:6-11.

God's word accomplishes what God sends it to do. We can trust that God's love will not reach out to us in vain: "For as the rain and the snow come down from heaven," says God, "so shall my word be . . . ; it shall not return to me empty!"

Isaiah's listeners were an agrarian people. They knew the cycle of the seasons and that rain and snow usually meant a fruitful harvest. Isaiah was not giving them a farming lesson; he was reminding them that they could depend upon God's word to get out to all creation and to produce astounding abundance.

Sometimes we would rather not have to think about effectiveness. We would prefer to keep the gospel at the level of speech, not action. That way we can feel we have done something if we merely talk about food for the hungry, shelter for the homeless, and countless other justice issues too close to home.

But God's word is the message of who God is through what God does in our midst. For God, word *is* action. It changes events and people. Whenever God speaks, life is transformed.

"For my thoughts are not your thoughts, nor are your ways my ways, says the Lord. . . . [My word] shall not return to me empty, but it shall accomplish that which I purpose, and succeed in the thing for which I sent it." What reassurance! We may muddle through good intentions and unfinished dreams with prayers that fizzle on the follow-through. But God's word endures, transforms us and all creation, and ultimately accomplishes its purpose!

—Betsy Schwarzentraub

✝ Thanks be to thee, O Lord Jesus Christ, for all the benefits which thou hast given us; for all the pains and insults which thou hast borne for us.

O most merciful Redeemer, friend, and brother, may we know thee more clearly, love thee more dearly, and follow thee more nearly, for thine own sake. Amen.

—Richard of Chichester, 13th century

✝ Read Psalm 139:7-12.

God's presence is not to be experienced only through the human heart and spirit. Indeed, all of creation gives witness to God's infinite and eternal dwelling in our midst. The psalmist recognizes that even a conscious effort to separate self from the Holy would be to no avail; for the heaven, the morning, the uttermost parts of the sea, darkness and light alike—even the remote abyss of Sheol—would declare that God is all around. And how is the psalmist encountered by God? The psalmist's own testimony is that God's extended hand leads him and God's right hand holds him.

What a blessing it is to know that the discerning of God's presence is not left simply to our own ability to find God. I am painfully aware of moments in my own life when I felt that God was absent and nowhere to be found. But always there has been a fellow or sister creature of God's handiwork who has helped me in my times of disbelief, bringing God close to me. I recall a rainstorm upon a cotton field that assured my tired body and weary spirit that God had not forgotten us sons and daughters, a bright sunlit morning that broke through the shadows of death with God's love, and a cool dusk that helped me to know God's presence in the turmoil of a failed marriage. Sisters and brothers, sometimes unbeknownst to them, have also at important moments provided just the right word of expression of care to affirm God's presence in my life. Yes! In all things, in all places and spaces under God's creation, God is present!

—Minerva G. Carcaño

✝ Read Psalm 126.

Sometimes new directions begin with tears. We must leave something behind, make a sacrifice, or face some unanticipated difficulty.

Most of the exiled community in Babylon chose to protect themselves from being stirred by a "path in the wilderness." Called to shake off seventy years of habit, they declined to find inner resources to face resettling Judea. Returning to Zion involved tears they were unwilling to shed—and laughter they would never know. For those who did return, life was more difficult than the stirring prophetic songs had led them to believe.

In this psalm, the returned exiles face a time of difficulty with tears, demands, and an affirmation: Those who sow in tears reap with shouts of joy.

The psalmist alludes to the ancient custom of ritual weeping during the sowing of the seed. The tears had originally been for the hidden divinity in the wheat, which must fall into the ground and die to make new life (see John 12:24). They were also a magical invitation for the rain to fall.

In this once-pagan custom the psalmist sees an affirmation of God's way with us: dealing with what is rather than what might have been is essential to honest spirituality. Rather than singing the prophet's songs to keep their spirits up, the people are called to "sow with tears."

Much spirituality involves pining for an idealized life rather than finding God in the hard edges and unexpected surprises of where—and who—we are. Our real responses to life are the stuff out of which strong souls can be grown.

—Robert Corin Morris

✝ Our Wednesday night Bible study group has become a rather odd community of sorts. We gather about 5:15 p.m. and share whatever food people have been able to bring. While we eat, we share joys and sorrows, celebrations and concerns, and all the stuff that falls in between. There are usually six to ten of us— two or three people who are struggling with mental health problems, three men who are homeless, several dealing with time in prison, and others wrestling with emotional and physical scars. Folks come with a hunger for healing, wanting food for the body and soul, and a place to be at home.

After eating, we take turns reading one or two of the lectionary passages and sharing whatever comes to mind as we try to discern words of challenge and comfort, words that might feed us anew.

John, one of the men who is currently homeless and staying, as the others who are homeless do, at the downtown mission, started out one night: "I got to tell a story on my own self. Happened this morning. See, I been trying so hard to live this new life. To stay clean. I just am really trying, for the first time, to live this stuff out. Some of you don't know how I used to live—drinking, drugging, knocking folks around. I always did read the Bible, but I just did it to put other folks down—quote stuff I wanted and go on about my business. It didn't mean nothing then. But it do now. And it's hard. It really is hard to live this stuff out. And sometimes it seems the more I try, the harder it gets.

"Stayed down at the mission again last night—house of pain for real. Woke up this morning and my shoes were gone. Somebody stole my shoes. I didn't even have to think about what to do—I pulled out my knife and I went looking. I was walking all up and down the dining hall, table by table, and I meant to get my shoes back. Kept thinking: in the old days wouldn't anybody tried to touch my shoes—'cause they'd know I'd get 'em 'fore they could ever put 'em on. Oh yeah. I was mean and folks knew it. Didn't care. And that's how it was this morning. It's one thing to give up drinking and drugging. It's another thing when they steal your shoes.

"And I'm hollering, threatening, and walking up and down

with my knife out where everyone can see. I'm going to get my shoes. Then old Jim here (points to another homeless man in the group) starts hollering from the other side of the room: 'Bible says if they take one cloak give them your other one; if they took your shoes, give 'em your socks. Put that knife away and give 'em your socks.'

"And I'm swearing and getting madder. Ain't givin' nobody nothin'! I want my shoes! And old Jim, he just keeps hollering: 'Give 'em your socks, John!'

"Folded up my knife. Took a long time doing it, too. Walked barefoot to the service center this morning—and got me some more shoes—but ain't it hard to live this stuff out!"

—Janet Wolf

✝ Read 2 Corinthians 4:16-18; 5:1.

Robert Louis Stevenson tells the story of an old garbage collector who lived and worked in the town dump. One day, someone who saw him at the dump expressed great concern about the man's working conditions. He replied, "Sir, he that has something ayont (beyond) needs never weary."

When we allow God's ways to take precedence in our lives, "we do not lose heart," because "our inner nature is being renewed everyday" (v. 16). Therefore, we do not grow weary. On the other hand, when we do not have faith in God or in a future life, when we know nothing about Jesus, when our world view is that of a mechanical process without any spiritual values, then the difficulties of daily living will influence our whole outlook. Then trouble will seem to be disaster; pain, calamity; and sorrow, tragedy.

For Paul, the experience with the living Christ transforms his entire being. This transformation brings meaning to Paul's statement in 4:18 and 5:1, a statement that immediately changes our whole understanding of this passage. Previously, Paul has been trying to place the "moment" in the context of "eternity" and the "visible" in the context of the "invisible." "We look not at what can be seen," he writes, "but at what cannot be seen." In other words, we no longer look forward to an "earthly house" but to "a house not made with hands, eternal in the heavens."

Because we look for that "ayont"—that beyond—we do not "grow weary in well-doing." That certainly is what gives us the confidence to follow the ways of our God.

—D. S. Dharmapalan

✝ Christ has no body now on earth but yours;
yours are the only hands with which he can do his work,
yours are the only feet with which he can go about the
world.
Yours are the only eyes through which his compassion
can shine forth upon a troubled world.
Christ has no body now on earth but yours.

—Teresa of Avila (1515-1582)

✝ There is a telling scene in the film *In Remembrance*. In this portrayal of the Last Supper, Jesus announces that the disciple who will betray him is the one whose hand is on the table. As the camera pans each disciple, one has a look of surprise, another a look of concern, yet another a look of questioning. And each disciple has a hand on the table. The visuals, whether reflective of the literal truth or indicative of the spiritual truth, imply that each one was capable of betraying Jesus.

Each disciple knew in some way that the seeds of betrayal are buried in each heart and that the bonds of loyalty can be weak even in the strongest of relationships. At that point, it was simply not clear to them who would betray Jesus. Each one was suspect.

Yet Jesus did not abandon them. He showed loyalty and compassion by staying at the table with them. Each one of these disciples, even Judas, was given to him by the heavenly Father as an answer to prayer (see Luke 6:12-16). In the midst of their questions about themselves and one another, Jesus refused to abandon them. Even knowing Judas' plans, Jesus washed his feet (John 13:5-20) and offered him bread to give him strength to change his mind (v. 26). As Ray Anderson in *The Gospel According to Judas* notes, "The grace of being chosen and loved by God counts more than the sin of betrayal."[1] Jesus will not let go of his own.

Our hands are on the table too. We are capable of betrayal through actions, words spoken and unspoken, and attitudes. Yet Jesus does not leave our table. He has called us and will not let us go.

—K. Cherie Jones

---

[1] Ray S. Anderson, *The Gospel According to Judas* (Colorado Springs: Helmers & Howard Publishers, 1991).

✝ Lord, let the pattern of my life,
    the course of my days,
be inexplicable apart from the intervention
    of the Risen One.
Let Jesus Christ be the sole justification
    for my life.

—Michel Bouttier

✝ Read Psalm 23.

It's Saturday, a good day to go to my local "do-it-yourself" hardware store and buy needed materials for fixing up this and that around the house. Doing it the "American" way—by myself. We like to describe ourselves as self-made men and women. We take pride in what we've achieved for ourselves.

Many of us approach the Lord in the same way. The Lord is the one who gives us the encouragement, or the insight, or whatever we need to "do it ourselves," spiritually speaking. We are basically competent, able, powerful people who have responsibility for ourselves. Please, Lord, I would rather do it myself.

Which makes all the more amazing that our favorite psalm is this one, Psalm 23. Here, there is no self-help, pull-yourself-up-by-your-bootstraps theology. Here, the Shepherd, the loving Shepherd, does it all. The verbs all point to loving actions by the Shepherd. The Shepherd makes, leads, restores, prepares, anoints, follows. We are the passive sheep, dependent upon the initiative and the care of the active Shepherd.

Psalm 23 is, therefore, the one we remember from our childhood. In the days of our childhood, when the world was confusing and we felt small and vulnerable, we learned this psalm by heart. As a pastor I've noted that when a person's life is drawing to a close, Psalm 23 is the last scripture most can remember, the gentle Shepherd leading us even through the darkest valley.

In this psalm, even we allegedly strong, assertive, self-confident ones learn to pray a better prayer: Please, Lord, do for me what I can't do for myself. Amen.

—William H. Willimon

✝ God be in my head
and in my understanding;
God be in my eyes
and in my looking;
God be in my mouth
and in my speaking;
God be in my heart
and in my thinking;
God be at my end
and at my departing.

—Sarum Primer (1514?)

✝ Read Isaiah 43:16-21.

God is a trailblazer inviting us to pioneer the future.

The Judean community in Babylonian exile is holding on for dear life to the ancestral past, hoping for the restoration of the old kingdom. The voice of this radical prophet interrupts their fearful nostalgia: stop relying on memories of God's way "in the sea" during the old Exodus. Prepare for the new Exodus of your own lifetimes: "I am about to do a new thing . . . I will make a way in the wilderness." We do not find the God of the Bible by keeping our noses stuck in a book but by writing the book's stories so deeply on our hearts that we, too, are able to see into the depths of the present moment.

The prophet challenges the exiles to get ready for a whole new world situation. A different kind of international society is dawning with the Persian Empire. With it comes the task of seeing and serving God in ways that will challenge the old tribal ways. Israel's concern is to be for the life of the world, not just for its own safety and prosperity.

The prophet summons a people caught between nostalgia for the past and the difficulty of coping with the Babylonian culture in which they are forced to live. A new trail can force our souls, like theirs were, to meet new challenges, evoking from within us new strengths previously dormant.

—Robert Corin Morris

✝ Read Luke 16:19-26.

The children of Somalia. The elderly and the children in Bosnia-Herzegovina. The victims of a drive-by shooting. The little girl abducted from her home and murdered by a stranger. Natural disasters such as floods, hurricanes, and earthquakes add to the suffering. The radical suffering of the world makes no sense. Does it really help to affirm that Lazarus was carried by the angels to Abraham's bosom? For Lazarus did not get better, and making a song of his angelic end does not diminish the real and relentless pain he experienced.

Even as you read this you can image a present human torment from which there is no surcease. Strategies of response are not curative; compassionate thoughts do not diminish real suffering.

Even so, for those of us who would seek to persist faithfully in the midst of the sufferings of history there are possibilities. We do not turn away and refuse to see in order to avoid the reality of suffering without sense of ease. In our faithfulness we risk seeing radical suffering and being present to it, even to the point of recognizing our own finitude and helplessness. It is positive not to avoid such pain, just as it is positive to acknowledge that there is no instant cure for human suffering.

To refuse to see it, to turn away, to sentimentalize or place easy blame does not help. What does? Presence, persistence, and small acts of resisitance in our own places count. These are the virtues of the faithful in a suffering world. Without them, we may sentimentalize, run away mad, or burn out.

—Peggy Ann Way

✝ Read Colossians 1:15-20.

Paul reminds us in these verses that Christ crucified overcomes our alienation from God's gracious love. Nevertheless, the atoning power of the cross requires us continually to turn our hearts toward the hope held before us in the gospel. The greatest mystery the world has ever known, says Paul, is the mystery of "Christ in you, the hope of glory" (NIV). You, once tarnished by despair, are now God's living expression of a promise awaiting all people.

Pause before the weight of this mystery of "Christ in you, the hope of glory." Can you, like Paul and the countless saints who have followed in his footsteps, recognize Christ's glory shining deep within you? Can you hear his eternal word of hope in the face of life's difficulties?

While you may feel discounted by the world, there is a resounding voice of truth whispering within your heart. You have been given the One whose name "is above every name" (Phil. 2:9, NIV)— and his name is written into the fabric of your soul. It is a name before which all creatures on heaven and earth shall bow, and it dwells deep within you, waiting to bring power and purpose to your life.

Today, begin your day by giving Christ the honor due his name. Grasp the hope within your heart, no matter how small or withered that hope may seem, and see if God will not fill you to overflowing with the only glory worth hoping for.

—Barry Stater-West

Week 5: A Time of Hope

I. **Prayer of Invitation**
Loving teacher, come and make your home in my heart this day and always. Dwell within me to save me from error and foolish ways. Teach me how to avoid doing harm this day and how to be an answer to another's prayer and help me today to be one of your signs of hope in the world. Stay with me always I pray, in the name of Jesus. Amen.

II. **Hymn of Praise:** "Lift High the Cross" (*UMH*, No. 159)

III. **Scripture Reading**
Sunday	John 20:19-31
Monday	John 21:1-14
Tuesday	Luke 24:36-53
Wednesday	Matthew 28:16-20
Thursday	John 21:15-19
Friday	Acts 1:1-14
Saturday	Acts 2:37-47

IV. **Reflection and Response**

V. **Sacred Reading**

VI. **Reflection and Response**

VII. **Prayer**
Thanksgiving for the signs of hope in the world and in the Church.
Petitions for:
   All leaders, especially those who seek to follow the path of righteousness, justice, and love;
   Persons in all walks of life, young and old, in every part of the world who seek to be obedient to the vision of God's reign and the unity of all humankind.
   Those in this congregation who seek only God's will in all the decisions we must make.

VIII.   **The Lord's Prayer**

IX.   **Closing Prayer of Consecration**
Gracious guide and giver of life and hope, I give you thanks for your steadfast love that has sustained me from before my birth and has brought me to this moment. I offer my life to you this day and invite you to guide, direct, and uphold me all day long. In the name of Jesus. Amen.

Readings for Reflection

✝ A Time of Hope

Hope has always been a dominant quality in the life of the Christian community. From the time of the resurrection of Jesus until today, individual Christians and the Christian community have been full of hope. In the face of fierce opposition and persecution, followers of Jesus never lost hope. Even when failure interrupted their journey, hope was the undercurrent that swept them to repentance, forgiveness, and companionship with the living Lord once more.

The source of this resolute hope was never found in the surroundings or how things were going for the Church. Rather, hope was found in God and the assurance that God was at work in the Church and in the world. The disciples felt a calm confidence that God's work and will would ultimately be completed and fulfilled. And they were assured that every Christian was invited into a partnership with God that moved toward the fulfillment of God's grand design for all creation. Such assurance is fertile ground in which the seeds of hope can flourish and bear the fruit of faithful living.

This week's readings give evidence of God's active presence within the Christian community. The Church is seen as the Body of Christ in the world, and individual Christians are seen as essential members of Christ's Body in the world. God is described as a near and present partner in all of life's experiences.

At times the near and present partner was rejected, and the Church became the crucified body of Christ all over again. There were times in the past and may be times for each of us when we think it too risky to be in partnership with God. We don't want to be the Body of Christ. We don't want to be too close to Jesus.

Sometimes we are just too shy, and sometimes we are reluctant to ask God to enter our decision making because we already know that our will must be surrendered to God's will. When we strongly hold a position that we think may not be God's will, we find difficulty asking God to enter our lives.

At times we may be like the child who wrote a letter to Jesus saying, "Please come to our house, we need you." Yet at other times we are not so sure we want to expose our motives, our desires, our wishes, and even our acts to the loving scrutiny of God. We quickly forget that God already knows and, even now, waits for our invitation to join with us in the work of personal and social transformation that leads to righteousness—righteousness that is a sign of God's reign and a sign of hope.

To remember that God's will shall be accomplished completely and that we are invited to be a part of the fulfillment of that will gives a new perspective to life. We lose some of our fear of the risk of seeking and doing God's will. We know that sometimes doing God's will does get us into trouble, and at other times it saves us from trouble. Most of all we know that, when we seek to know and do God's will, we have set our feet upon a pathway of companionship, joy, and fulfillment. Our journey becomes one that holds challenge, excitement, meaning, assurance, and deep peace. Our journey gets richer day by day and will never end. Our journey begins in this life and continues into the next. Our journey is made possible by the One who walks with all those who are faithful.

A Christian or a Christian community eagerly and sincerely seeking God's companionship and direction is a wonderful sign of hope. With God's help and our desire, we can be that sign of hope to others today.

—Rueben P. Job

✝ We are just beginning to understand ecology, the idea that we all live in interrelated, balanced systems. Interfering with rain forests in Brazil affects our climate in the United States, and our search for air-conditioned comfort is destroying a protective layer of atmospheric ozone. We are just now learning to look for the balances.

The early Christians of Jerusalem seem to have found, in the fellowship of the risen Lord, a way to balance their social system within the group. Indeed, evidence suggests this was their best witness to the resurrection—that those who knew Christ alive in them could also find the love to meet the needs of one another.

This was their one heart and soul, that all belonged to God, that all they had was at Christ's disposal, and that it was a joy to help out if they could. It was in this community that the Easter message was shared. Christ is alive, still catching the love of people today and changing them. But how? By the fellowship community of the believers, by the Church.

Our witness today may lack the power we have read about, but the machinery is still in place. As we look for the balances of nature, we look, too, for the fellowship of the believers because it is there that the living, resurrected Christ visits most often.

If we are to meet Jesus ourselves, we must seek out that gathering of the saints. Ever since that first Easter, Christ has been in their midst.

—John Clifford

✝ Read 1 Corinthians 15:12-20.

Without Christ there was no hope in my life. Although I had fulfilled society's demands by earning a doctoral degree from Harvard, teaching at the state university, and presenting the status those provided, my life was empty. The promise of resurrection, of a new life in Jesus Christ, transformed my life from a hate-filled life to a life searching for peace, justice, and service to others. It was like the story of the Hebrew scriptures: one paradise lost (Eden) and another gained (the promised land). In Christ, there is no longer confusion: He was raised from the dead as an affirmation that the resurrection, a new life in Jesus Christ, is available to all of those who believe (John 11:25-26).

The problem with many of us Christians today, as it was when Paul wrote to the Corinthians, is that we are unable to imagine how any kind of existence can be possible after death. This problem poses a predicament for us, for if there is no resurrection, there is no reason for our faith. If that is the case, argues Paul, then there is no forgiveness of sins and salvation is an illusion. Thus, there is no transformation possible through grace, only through deeds.

The need to believe is clear. If God can transform an intellectual nonbeliever into a new creature (2 Cor. 5:17), then Resurrection took place and Jesus was the "first fruit." Look inside yourself: In how many ways has God transformed you? How is God transforming you right now?

—Juan G. Feliciano

✝ The key to winning at tug-of-war lies not in the bulk of the team (though that helps) but in how well the team members can pull together, how well–synchronized they can be. When all the members pull and brace together, they will be hard to overcome.

That is how Luke describes the early church in Jerusalem (Acts 4:32-33). They are all of one heart and soul, totally committed to the work of the group. They are pulling together.

Now Luke adds an evaluation here. Because of this, the company of apostles has great power and great grace. But notice that it happens only in the heart of the fellowship.

Like a nuclear reactor that needs a critical mass of fuel, the church needs to gather Christ's followers into a critical mass of fellowship—one in heart and soul and purpose—before that great power can be generated.

Once that happens—look out! We speak of the growth of the church at this stage as explosive. It spreads in all directions and nothing can hold it in. New followers join the fellowship, experience for themselves the presence of the risen Lord, and set out to share that marvelous experience with their friends.

Where this unleashed power is channeled to preaching Christ, one more effect appears. "Great grace was upon them all" (Acts 4:33). Grace, the blessing of God's love and Christ's forgiveness, the renewing work of God in a multitude of lives, becomes visible to the world.

—John Clifford

✝ In the luminous story of the walk to Emmaus, the risen Jesus joins two of his friends on the road. They do not recognize him at first but share their grief over the suffering and death of Jesus, which had disappointed their hopes that he would redeem Israel. As they walk, he talks with them, opening new depths and understanding of the scriptures, bringing meaning to the suffering. They invite him to the inn; he sits with them at table, blesses, breaks, and gives the bread. In that act they know him. But when he leaves their sight, they wonder together why they had not recognized him earlier. "Were not our hearts burning within us while he was talking to us on the road?" (Luke 24:32).

As I reread this story, I realized that this burning of the heart actually accompanies each of the major steps of discernment. It is the signal for each qualitative shift, every deepening of perception and recognition. When I understand something about myself I had not seen before, when I face what I really feel and where I really want to go, when I see my traps, false prophets, idols for what they really are, when my hidden treasure, the buried gift, opens before me, my heart burns. For me, it has become the true sign that Christ's Spirit is "talking to me on the road." I am suspicious of any serious choices, commitments, relationships which are not accompanied by the deep inner burning of the heart's recognition.

But can this inner fire be trusted as the authentic sign? After all, any deceived lover, any cult member, any former ideologue could well say: "My heart burned too—at the beginning." I think we need to "unpack" this experience of the burning heart. We need to see and test its contents and characteristics. What emerges is very different from the fire of the "father of lies" which first obscures our clear sight by its conflagration, violates our free choice, and leaves us with ashes. It is worthwhile to read the whole story of the Emmaus encounter to the end of the chapter, which also concludes the Gospel of Luke.

The two friends return to Jerusalem and share their experience with the other disciples. The presence of Jesus stands among them again. As we study closely the account, we see clearly delineated the nature of the fire that burned in their hearts. Peace was spoken in their midst. Authentic clarity was given. Redemptive meaning was given to pain. Fear was healed, and joy was released and increased. Jesus was shown to them as one who shares the full human condition and who is resurrected in the midst of his humanity, and theirs. Empowerment from God was promised rather than demands for their will power. Above all, the whole encounter was drenched with the spirit of tenderness, the burning love which is released from fear. And this is the supreme sign, the authentic, unmistakable presence of the Spirit we call Holy.

> Beloved, let us love one another,
> because love is from God. . . .
> If we love one another, God lives in us,
> and his love is perfected in us.
> By this we know that we abide in him and he in us,
> because he has given us of his Spirit. . . .
> There is no fear in love, but perfect love casts out fear;
> for fear has to do with punishment. . . .
> We love because he first loved us.
>   (1 John 4:7, 12-13, 18-19)

And by this sign of love we are healed of fear, and we know when Christ's Spirit is "talking to us on the road." This is our one infallible fire.

—Flora S. Wuellner

✝ Read Genesis 15:4-12, 17-18.

It is not hard to understand how hopeless Abraham felt when contemplating his childlessness. Like Abraham, we are often confronted with seemingly insurmountable challenges. Like him, we sometimes feel as if God is either blind to our needs or powerless to assist us. The more desperate the situation, the worse we feel. A sick and aging parent, a rift in our marriage, prolonged unemployment, a troubled child—why doesn't God see that we need help?

We are so much like Abraham that his words sound familiar. "What can you give me?" The question has a hollow, self-pitying ring. If we repeat it several times, we can fully grasp the bitterness and failure it expresses.

God's reply to the question was not meant only as a comfort to Abraham. It was also a foreshadowing, an example of God preparing the people for the Sinai covenant. "Look toward heaven and count the stars . . . . So shall your descendants be." God wanted Abraham's people to know that they were chosen; he could not have used a better metaphor. To say to that childless man that he will have as many descendants as there are stars in the sky reveals God's understanding of Abraham's despair and God's desire to comfort Abraham.

In God's reassurance of Abraham, there is a message for us. God's response to "What can you give me?" recalls Abraham's deliverance. As God heard Abraham, so God hears us; and God will keep the covenant with us as well.

—Judith Freeman Clark

✝ In his gentle way Jesus comes into the company of two walking to Emmaus. He presumes nothing, but simply joins them since safety in numbers was common for travelers. When occasion presents itself, Jesus shares his good news. At village edge, he hints at going on but accepts their offer of hospitality. Luke gives no indication that Jesus is yet recognized (see Luke 24:13-35).

The economy of details leaves a lot of the story to our imagining. We depend on studying translations and commentaries for details. J. B. Phillips translates the key event by giving this emphasis in verse 31: *"Then it happened!"*[1] When Jesus was at table with them, he took bread, gave thanks, broke it, and handed it to them. In that most common of daily privileges—breaking bread—their eyes were opened.

Perhaps they were among the five thousand when Jesus broke bread, or perhaps they had heard him say, "I am the bread of life" (John 6:35). Whatever the reason for their recognizing that Emmaus moment, Jesus became present. Then they understood why it had been like fire burning within them as he had explained the scriptures to them.

John Wesley was listening to scripture being explained on the evening of May 24, 1738. He wrote in his journal, "I felt my heart strangely warmed. I felt I did trust in Christ, Christ alone for salvation. And an assurance was given me, that he had taken away my sins." The assurance of the presence of the risen Christ bonds us to Christ and inspires us to reproduce his life in our faithful living.

—Robert K. Smyth

✝ I have certainly had those times in my life when I wanted to make sure God heard me clearly—the times when I was in some crisis, had a loved one very ill, or cared deeply about something. I tried to figure out some way to let God know these requests were especially urgent.

Yet as a parent, I want to listen carefully to all the joys, concerns, feelings, and requests of my own children in whatever state they are. Surely God is even more attentive than I as a human parent am able to be (though, of course, God has many more children than I). Perhaps the real issue here is my ability to trust that God hears and responds appropriately. Sometimes what I need is simply a chance to pull out feelings and thoughts and to look at them in God's presence.

Sometimes we are asked to be God's listening ear for someone else. We are called to listen with as much of the compassion and love of God as we can manage to have. Perhaps in those moments we will need to pray for help to listen well, to "incline our ears" toward this other person on God's behalf. Sometimes what that person may need is simply a chance to pull

---

[1] From THE NEW TESTAMENT IN MODERN ENGLISH © J. B. Phillips 1958. Used by permission of Macmillan Company.

out his or her thoughts and feelings and look at them. I have come to believe that when we really listen to one another, we are like God and the spirit of God dwells in us.

—Susan Ruach

✝ Lord, teach me to turn toward You,
    even if I don't yet know how to look at You.
    Lord, You are my strength,
    even if I don't know how to grasp You.
    Lord, You are my salvation,
    even if I don't know how to believe.
    Lord, You are my pardon,
    even if I no longer know how to repent.
    Lord, You are love,
    even if I don't know how to love.
        Praise be to You!

—Michel Bouttier

✝ Read Job 1:1-17; Psalm 22:1-2.
    I turned off the engine and the lights, rolled down the window, and told the kids to listen. The quiet starlit night covering the country road was refreshing to my city-cluttered ears. We were there less than a minute when one of the boys asked, "Are we gonna go now?"
    What I found to be solitude the children thought of as spooky. That which was irresistible to me was insecurity to them. In the dark, especially as children, we do not rest.
    Job was in the dark spiritually. A heavy, thick darkness had fallen upon him. He was afraid. The psalmist echoes the trembling voice of Job: "O my God, I cry out by day, but you do not answer, by night, and am not silent" (NIV).
    Darkness. How do you handle those ink-stained days; days none of us are immunized against? As a child I stared into the night, unable to sleep. Sometimes in desperation I cried and cried and cried. Like my son on the country road, we as adults tend to say to God when the shroud of darkness blinds our eyes, "Are we gonna go now?"
    Would it have seemed strange to hear Job ask that same question? In the dark I am frightened. Are we gonna go now, Lord? I have lost those dearest to me. Are we gonna go now? All the wealth of a lifetime has been snatched away. Are we gonna

go now? Lord, are we going to move on away from this place of ruin? Are we gonna go now?

But Job seems to have been blessed with night vision for his journey. Somehow he caught glimpses of light beyond the shadows of death. Through it all, Job was a man of hope.

—Charles R. Brown

✝ My hope is built on nothing less
than Jesus' blood and righteousness.
I dare not trust the sweetest frame,
but wholly lean on Jesus' name.

On Christ the solid rock I stand,
all other ground is sinking sand;
all other ground is sinking sand.

—Edward Mote, 1834

✝ Read Psalm 19:1-6.

And now here is another sort of word, one that goes beyond language. The whole universe makes a statement about its Creator. The pattern of the coming of light and dark, the changing seasons, the rhythm of birth and death and new life— the never-ending cycle of creation—is lived out year by year. In all of this we can see, if we are willing, the handiwork of God. There is nothing more powerful than the sun, and the daily rising of the sun has always been something which early people acknowledged with respect. This is something we sophisticated, modern, often urbane people should learn from. We should never take for granted this daily gift of God to us. Although we live with the assumption that the sun will rise daily, we should never allow ourselves to take this daily miracle for granted.

Perhaps we might think for a moment of what the sun will see on its daily circuit, that tabernacle (v. 4c) that God has made for it to run its course, the whole world, human and nonhuman alike, created just for this one thing: to give endless glory, praise, and thanksgiving to the generosity of the living creator God.

—Esther de Waal

✝ Jesus, joy of our desiring,
holy wisdom, love most bright;
drawn by thee, our souls aspiring
soar to uncreated light.

Word of God, our flesh that fashioned,
with the fire of life impassioned,
striving still to truth unknown,
soaring, dying round thy throne.

Through the way where hope is guiding,
hark, what peaceful music rings;
where the flock, in thee confiding,
drink of joy from deathless springs.
Theirs is beauty's fairest pleasure;
theirs is wisdom's holiest treasure.
Thou dost ever lead thine own
in the love of joys unknown.

—Martin Janus (1661)

✝ Read 1 Samuel 17:19-23, 32-49.

Christian, determined to make his way from the City of Destruction to the Celestial City, falls into the Slough of Despond. It is a bog, a swamp; and loaded with his sins as he is, Christian begins to sink.

The army of Israel stood in despondent fear before the might of Goliath. The saying goes that it is darkest before the dawn. That is often the time when, at the end of our rope, God's deliverance surprises us. And what an unlikely source provided God's deliverance for Israel—a lad, a keeper of sheep. Young David faced Goliath with fuzz still on his cheeks and an innocent trust in God in his heart. Hearing the taunting of Goliath, he offers himself as Israel's champion. At first Saul rejects the offer as ridiculous. Then he listens and finally agrees. Perhaps something in the lad's passion, in his confidence in God, won Saul's consent.

So David goes to face the giant. He has no heavy armor, no great spear—only a sling and five smooth stones from the brook. The giant roars in disbelieving laughter, as David's sling begins to circle. Then the Philistine champion falls and the rest is history.

No one escapes a sense of loss. Our own folly, hidden faults, a friend's betrayal, the loss of someone deeply loved, the failure of a dream, some seemingly senseless accident can cause us to sink in despair. In this time of loss, when we are at the end of our human resources, God will send deliverance. Wait for it. It will surely come. We are a resurrection people.

—Ron James

Week 6: A Living Companionship

I. **Prayer of Invitation**
God of all wisdom and truth, come to fill my life with your presence. Dispel the dark clouds of doubt and depression, reveal and remove that which is false from my life, help me to cast out all other gods and to live in loving companionship with you this day and always. Amen.

II. **Hymn of Praise:** "O Spirit of the Living God" (*UMH*, No. 539)

III. **Scripture Reading**

Sunday	Luke 24:13-35
Monday	Acts 9:1-9
Tuesday	Acts 9:10-19
Wednesday	Romans 12:1-8
Thursday	Romans 12:9-21
Friday	Romans 8:1-17
Saturday	Romans 8:18-39

IV. **Reflection and Response**

V. **Sacred Reading**

VI. **Reflection and Response**

VII. **Prayer**
Thanksgiving for God's leadership during all of life and especially during these past weeks of more intense efforts of discernment.
Petitions for:
All who seek the light of Christ for their darkness;
All who suffer the evils of addiction, oppression, and injustice;
All who are this day making decisions, especially the leaders of the church and the world who this day seek your will;
All who suffer and those who are dying, that none will suffer or die alone;

All who seek to live out their prayers and live into a closer walk with God.

VIII. **The Lord's Prayer**

IX. **Closing Prayer of Consecration**
Holy Spirit, guide and comforter of all who turn to you for help, thank you for your sustaining presence in the life of the Church and in my own life. I offer my life once more to your direction this day. Lead me wherever you will and sustain me wherever you lead me. Grant to me the necessary strength to walk in faithfulness and to live in company with you all day long. In the name of Jesus. Amen.

Readings for Reflection

✝ A Living Companionship

Discernment at its best is the consequence of a daily and life-time walk with God. A lifetime of such companionship produces profound results that range from guidance in decision making to transformation of one's life. Living a life of discernment, then, is a simple process of staying attentive to and open to God in all of the active and contemplative times of our lives.

Practicing preference for God has always been the first commandment and the first step toward faithful living. From this stance we seek God and God's companionship first. And as we do so, we will learn how to surrender our will to God's will. We will learn that God's presence and direction can be trusted. From this vantage point we learn that God's will is good and to be desired. When these truths begin to become a part of our very lives, discernment becomes a natural consequence of our daily walk with God.

When our preference is for God and God's will alone, we can begin to see the possibility of "indifference" in our own decision making. "Indifference" is the Ignatian term for the capacity to be free from prior commitments, to be genuinely open to God's will and God's leadership. This kind of freedom, essential to discernment and faithfulness, is very hard to discover in our own lives. We bring so many pre-conceived ideas and so many strongly held prejudices that must be removed before we can be open to receive some new word or direction from God. To further complicate our movement toward indifference is the constant bombardment of other views. Some are well intentioned, believed to be God's will by those who promote them. Others may have fallen into the unhealthy and unholy world of political power plays that result in winners and losers.

Therefore, to have a way of living with God that serves to remind us again and again who we are and who God is in our lives is important. Such a rhythm of life will include time and space for listening to the Word, periods of deep and intimate prayer, a sensitive listening to the cries of God's people, and an action cycle that leads to reconciling, healing, and saving deeds. This kind of living becomes an answer to our prayers.

Another reason a lifetime of companionship with the living God is the way to discernment is the time that it takes to develop relationships of trust. Time is necessary for such a relationship with God to develop and mature. We learn by practicing this life of companionship just as we learn how to seek and receive God's direction in all things. When small and seemingly insignificant decisions flow out of this companionship, we will find it will be natural for us to practice discernment and obedience to God's direction in the major decisions for our lives. "Whoever is faithful in a very little is faithful also in much; and whoever is dishonest in a very little is dishonest also in much" (Luke 16:10).

We know from experience that those who live together for long periods of time begin to think and act alike. Workers on an assembly line, team members of highly trained sports teams, or work teams with complex assignments often can anticipate the thoughts and actions of one another. We even learn to "read" our children, spouse, or siblings and know what they will do in any given situation. When we live with God in daily companionship and declare our first preference for God and God's will, we develop our natural capacity to know, live with, and follow God in all of life. Out of this kind of companionship true discernment arises most easily.

I suspect that your life, as mine, may not yet be at this ideal place of discernment. We may find lapses in our "indifference" and see our own will or that of another displace God as central in our lives. When we become aware of such lapses, we should not scold ourselves or give up on the concept of companionship with the living God. Rather, we must return once again to God, ask for help to walk faithfully, and go on confident that God understands our weakness, is pleased with our desire for companionship, and will offer assistance equal to our need.

Each of us has the capacity to discern God's will. The capacity to do God's will is developed as we practice a way of living that keeps us in companionship with God and faithful to God's direction in our daily lives. Gradually we learn to hear, see, and know God's direction more and more until our individual and corporate decision making flows out of our companionship with and clear preference for God.

—Rueben P. Job

✝ For centuries, as a community, we have sought the brush of wings, the assurance that God's life quickens in us. We have asked, Where do we look? What does it feel like? How do we listen? Will we know? And we have named this inner art of paying attention. We have called it "the discernment of spirits." Over the millennia, Christians have tried to hone the practice of this art, for it is seen to be at the core of the spiritual life. Although there are various methods or schools of thought on discernment, in general it might be said that discernment is about two things: attentiveness and discrimination.

All Christians are called to the spiritual life in the sense that we understand ourselves as a community empowered by the Spirit of God. We claim that the Spirit of God animates the church (recall the descent of the Spirit at Pentecost). We claim that Jesus promised to send a Comforter so that we would not be alone (recall his last discourses in the book of John). We claim that Jesus was so enspirited (recall his baptism in the Jordan and his proclamation of ministry). To be "spiritual" in the most ancient sense of the term means to be under the power of God's Spirit.[1]

From earliest times, Christians have claimed that the spiritual life is about paying attention to the Spirit moving in and among us and distinguishing that Spirit from the vast array of other "spirits" vying for our attention. These other spirits have been characterized as having a variety of origins: They may be spirits of the "world" (the purposes of normative culture that do not align with the purposes of God), spirits of the "flesh" (variously

---

[1] This is quite distinct from the way the term is often used today—to distinguish institutional and formal religious observance from observance that is perceived as more fervent and personally meaningful.

conceived as the addictive demands of bodily need or the egocentric demands of the self-absorbed life), or the spirit of the "evil one" (active forces working against good or the disordered meanderings of the human heart and mind that destroy and enslave rather than enliven and free). However the spirits are conceived, the Spirit of God is one touch, one inner brushing among many, and much of the work of the spiritual life consists in discerning which is which.

—Wendy M. Wright

✝ Read Psalm 81:12-16.

God says through the psalmist, "I gave them over to their stubborn hearts, to follow their own counsels." The stubborn hearts at Meribah—"Why did you bring us out of Egypt, to kill us . . . with thirst?" (Exod. 17:3). The "stiff-necked" people at Sinai—"Come, make gods for us" (Exod. 32:1).

There are stubborn hearts today. Mine is one. I identify with the people in the wilderness. I worry that there will not be enough, that I will lose my job, my security, my health. I want to do things *my* way so that I will be sure they get done and get done right.

Waiting on God, being patient and trusting that my needs will be provided for—that is not my strength. Why should I launch into a wilderness without provisions? Why should I trust a God I cannot see, a God who seems to always procrastinate until the last minute when coming to rescue me?

My stubborn heart wants to listen to God only when it fits into my plan. But God invites me to take risks, to listen to and follow God's leading. I may not be led where I thought I was going or receive the things I asked for.

Letting go of my stubborn heart means cultivating a relationship with God. It means trusting even when everything seems lost. The psalmist tells me that God will provide nourishment for those who will listen—I will be fed with the finest wheat and satisfied with the sweetest honey.

God invites me to let go of the control that creates a stubborn heart and a stiff neck in my day-to-day living.

—Beth A. Richardson

✝ Discernment requires that we pay attention. We must attend to both what goes on around us and within us. An attentive pregnant woman pays attention on many levels. She is aware of the need for proper food, rest, and exercise for her body which now must operate at peak capacity. She is aware, especially if she is a first-time mother, of the advice, stories, encouragement, and admonitions of doctors, relatives, and friends. She is aware of the changing configuration of her form, the new ways of moving and being required of her. She notes new thoughts and feelings, the dreams coming to be, the emerging fears, the changing relationships with her partner, parents, or siblings.

She realizes she is changing. Her sense of who she is is changing. She feels the dynamism of the strong other growing within her, its habits and cycles, its enlarging demands. Perhaps she is attentive to the mystery of life itself that impinges more and more on her ordinary consciousness: the God questions, the life and death questions, the deep joy and deep grieving questions.

Spiritual discernment asks us to pay attention. We need to attend to both what goes on around us and within us. Ideally, this attentiveness goes on much of the time, a sort of low level, constant spiritual sifting of the data of our experience. But there are times when discernment becomes much more focused, when a crossroad is reached or a choice called for. At times like these the cumulative wisdom of tradition tells us to pay attention on many levels: to consult scripture, to seek the advice of trusted advisors, to heed the *sensus fidelium* (the collective sense of the faithful), to read widely and deeply the best ancient and contemporary thinking, to pray, to attend to the prick of conscience and to the yearnings and dreamings of our hearts, to watch, to wait, to listen.

—Wendy M. Wright

✝ Meister Eckhart has said, "Our happiness, however, does not lie in our accomplishments, but rather in the fact that we undergo God." My glimpses of communal discernment are incomplete. I realize there is far more I need to understand. Yet even now I would cite this simple matter as among the most compelling marks of the discerning community and among the most moving: The discerning community of faith is, in Eckhart's phrase, undergoing God. God beckons. God draws forth. And as the community responds, even haltingly, God sustains. God permeates. God shapes. All this comes of God at once.

Such undergoing, as I have seen it, dawns where there is a gentle and graced willingness at the heart of the community of faith. This willingness is not wrapped in the expectations of instant change. It is not encased in tight mechanisms of control that would force a community in some direction already selected by its leaders. The willingness arises utterly unadorned. It is a modest, "Here we are." It is a "Let it be with us according to your will." It is a deep "Yes" to the new patterns of prayer, attentiveness, and communal understanding that emerge.

And the "Yes" to undergoing God invariably gives rise to patterns of living where love becomes incarnate. The changes are fresh and deep. In a church fellowship hall that once echoed with biting words of anger, some eighty persons of all ages now gather every Wednesday night to study, pray, and support one another in the lives of service they carry forth through the week. Not far from that fellowship hall a small congregation is being transformed by its ministry among persons who live with chronic mental illness. It is at times a challenging transformation, but at all points that community grows new.

Whenever I look on such matters as these, I see birth: God's new birth; God's life taking form among us. A community of faith that consciously discerns the fresh beckonings of God is also a community that undergoes God.

—Stephen V. Doughty

✝ Psalm 139 is a prayer of praise and thanksgiving which humbly acquiesces to God's personal knowledge of each of us. It helps us understand more clearly how intimately God is present to us.

The psalmist proclaims that God created him with infinite care and formed him in the divine likeness. Here and in Hebrews 4:13, the writer acknowledges God's wisdom which knows the attitudes and thoughts of the heart. God is so intimately present to us that nothing can be hidden.

For some this thought could be frightening, for it might project an ever-watchful God who scrutinizes and records all that we say and do. On the other hand, the certainty of God's presence can be joyful, for it underlines the care God has for us. Recognizing this God who is inside us nurturing us and outside us challenging us as we are enveloped by love can lead us to greatness as we live life fully and intensely.

As did the psalmist, visualize God as being present at your conception and your birth, pleased and joyful at the creation that is being brought forth. Do you feel the intensity of this pleasure, this joy, this love? Do you love yourself the way the Lord loves you?

Sometimes it is hard to see ourselves as God sees us, to love ourselves as God loves us. We have somehow learned to be afraid of God rather than to feel secure in God's presence. To love ourselves as God loves us means learning to trust that the God who created us is the One who will never let us go.

—Loretta Girzaitis

✝ All of us are called to discipleship, and all are free to accept or reject it. If we accept, Jesus tells us we must deny ourselves and take up our cross daily and follow him.

Basically, taking up the cross means a freely chosen denial of ourselves in service of God. This is giving up some control over our destiny and opening ourselves to true self-knowledge so that we might give up some of our illusions about the world, about messiahship, about power. It means letting ourselves be shaped by Jesus. And the context of all this is the family, the church, the neighborhood, the nation, and the world.

We don't go out seeking the cross, but we know that following Jesus in service of God—which involves meeting human needs—involves walking on a path that has crosses, prices, pain, and hurt that must be accepted. Sometimes our true crosses are difficult to recognize. I might think my cross is a chronic disease when the true cross might be accepting my loss of independence or control over my life. I might see my cross as loneliness when my true cross is giving up the insatiable demand for attention and affection that controls my life so that I miss the loving attention given to me daily. Or I might reject the crosses that come my way because I am so taken up with the crosses of others. The hardest thing is to carry my own cross. If I cannot carry what is uniquely mine while I agonize over the pain of others, am I a true disciple? If I really want to form a bond with those who suffer oppression of any kind, must I not first, or at least simultaneously, suffer my own pain, whatever it might be?

And as always, just as Jesus carried his cross for all of us together, so we carry our crosses together.

—Stefanie Weisgram

✝ Read Psalm 139:1-6.

How many people can we say really know us? We are a mobile culture and have less time to become well-acquainted with people in our community.

My daughter and I have moved from one city to another several times within the span of a few years. Whenever we were beginning to know a city—the best shops, where children could eat free, a church home—we had to move. Each move provided a better opportunity for us, but we found ourselves alone at first, having to get to know our community all over again. I sometimes regret that my daughter will not have the same experience I had growing up. I lived in the same house, went to the same stores, knew everyone's business in the neighborhood until I left for college. I miss that for my daughter.

However, the psalmist tells us that we are never really alone—even when we're strangers in a new city. We have a God who is in relationship with us. We can be assured that God knows us with the wonderful knowledge of intimacy. We are surrounded by the presence of God. God takes the time to know us. We know God through our relationships with one another.

Therefore, we are not to try to look for a God so big, so cosmic that we miss God right in front of us. If we look across at our neighbor, around at creation, and within ourselves we will discover the presence of God.

—Hilda R. Davis

✝ After experiencing the risen Christ and receiving the Holy Spirit, the believers in Jerusalem experienced unity. The account in Acts 4:32-35 is reminiscent of Psalm 133. Wherever Christians were throughout the city, they experienced a bond of caring, a common vision of how to live a Christian life. The risen Christ is never just for us to receive; we must also do our part by sharing with others out of the foundation of that experience.

Sharing is a community phenomenon with external and internal components. The external manifestation of sharing God's grace in the Jerusalem community was the sharing of property. Those who had property sold it when needed for the benefit of the entire community because their identity was found in the community rather than in individual property. The community was held in high esteem because its members were never needy.

The internal component that motivated the sharing of property was the sharing of themselves. When individuals gather with their identities based on individual achievements and possessions, the result is people hiding their needs or pretending to be something they are not. When a community gathers with its identity found in the well-being of the entire group, then people are more willing to share themselves, to be vulnerable, and to express their needs.

Communities form around a variety of shared interests or causes. Christian communities are drawn together in the experience of the risen Christ. The risen Christ unites us heart and soul, enabling us to overcome our isolation as individuals and become the people of God.

—Phyllis R. Pleasants

✝ May you each day and every moment, in the fellowship of Jesus' sufferings and sharing His
feelings, bury all that threatens to confound you in
your ministry. May you be granted each moment to
measure up to His pardon, His power, and to the
royal achievement of love—and thus, half hidden,
half visible, to see traced across the enigmatic
geography of your parish, the real foundation of the
Kingdom of God.

—Michel Bouttier

✝ Read Luke 15:1-7.

The moral of this moving parable is clearly that the Good Shepherd will go to any length to save the lost sheep!

Jesus rebukes the Pharisees, who neglect the most needy, but he offers encouragement and hope to the penitent. The Pharisee would ignore the sinner. Not God! The Pharisee saw no hope for the sinner. Not God!

In Alfred Soord's painting The Lost Sheep, for whatever reason—curiosity, adventure, eating its way from the flock—the sheep is clinging to the edge of a cliff, bleating for help. In the fast-approaching night, birds of prey circle overhead, waiting. The shepherd finds it! He hangs on to a ledge with one hand and reaches down with the other to grasp the sheep.

A couple of thoughts come to mind. God loves the sinner no matter what the sin. And there is no room for hopelessness in

God's love. Every soul is precious. As the well-known poem by Francis Thompson points out so well, "The Hound of Heaven" seeks us in our lostness until we discover him! All the energy of heaven is released to find even the one poor, wandering soul.

People tried to hide from God by burying Jesus in a tomb, but God broke the lock and released him! He is still—still!—alive in our contemporary world.

In our own unique journey, we can become so intent on personal desires that we do not hear the voice of God calling our name or see the hand of God reaching out to us. Yet, in the depths of the heart there is a still, small voice that cries for help, and there is another still, small Voice that replies, "I have found my sheep!"

—John W. Bardsley

✝ Read Psalm 30.

In its poetry, this psalm speaks of human suffering, healing, thanksgiving, and praise. In the process the psalmist tells us something of what God is like.

Someone has suffered from a very serious illness. To describe the misery, the psalmist likens it to being in Sheol or the Pit, meaning, in the realm of the dead.

There are many experiences in life that feel like being in the realm of the dead. There are times when we seem to be moving more toward death than toward life. The power of death is anything that blocks our growth and development. It is being stuck, held down, having our breath knocked out of us. Or, as one of my favorite people used to say, "It's like getting stuck in Good Friday and never moving on to Easter morning."

The psalmist gives thanks to God for rescue and deliverance from the realm of the dead, for restoration to life. In praise, the psalmist tells us what God chooses for us—life. God's anger is brief; God's favor forever. Weeping is part of life, but joy comes in God's morning. God's will for us is not mourning and sorrow. God would clothe us in garments of joy and rejoicing. God invites us to take off that sackcloth and move onto the dance floor.

God is with us when we feel like we are living in the realm of death. God is with us even in death. Yet God is still the God of life. The psalmist tells us and the Resurrection shows us that God prefers life.

—Linda Johnson

✝ Read Psalm 145:17-21.

When a friend of mine was going through a divorce, she said, "I never felt further from the church or closer to God." In her church community she felt judged and, at times, rejected. When she turned to God, she found understanding and unconditional love.

I have also heard people in grief support groups say that during their most intense mourning, the church was not a comfort to them. I don't believe they are saying—nor am I implying—that the clergy and their congregations lack compassion or are indifferent to the suffering among them. Sometimes the grieving do not attend church because it is too painful a reminder of the funeral and all that they have lost. Others fail to ask the church for help that would be forthcoming if they made their needs known.

Because some people who are hurting do not find solace in their church does not mean they have distanced themselves from God. Quite the contrary. During periods of emotional pain, many people say that they have never been so prayerful or felt so deeply spiritual. What they discover is the God the psalmist praises in today's reading: the God who hears their cry; the God who is just and kind; the God who is near to all who call out. However dark their thoughts, however bleak their spirit, however angry or sad or hopeless they feel, God does not condemn or judge. God listens and loves them nonetheless.

—Mary Montgomery

✝ Read Psalm 63:6-8.

In the silence of the night, all our roles and pretenses slip away, leaving us vulnerable and alone. Occasionally tears, regrets, or anxieties can creep into our beds as we lie awake trying to sort through a jumble of loneliness, confusion, or shame.

The psalms give us a language for such times of anguish and for the grace that shines through them. It is precisely in these moments of weakness or worry that God's life-giving presence upholds us and gives us hope. In the darkest nights of our soul's need, God can turn our tears into joy.

"I think of you on my bed, and meditate on you in the watches of the night," says Psalm 63 (verse 6). As we lie awake in the dark with all masks stripped away, God's sheer grace upholds us. Like a newborn clutching its mother, we cling for life to God's love for us, as we are, no matter what our failures or faults.

"You have been my help. In the shadow of your wings I sing for joy!" As shade is welcome in an arid land, so do we find the shadow of God's presence in our self-scorched souls (Psalm 121:5). As a hen gathers helpless chicks under her wings for protection and comfort, so God seeks to gather us (Matt. 23:37).

"My soul clings to you," we cry out in the middle of our own deepest nights. And we sing, "Your right hand upholds me!"

In our sleepless times of mortality and unknowing, the uncertainty or woundedness in our lives causes us to admit our creatureliness. It is in such a "dark night of the soul" that God's loving presence enfolds us, and we can sing for joy.

—Betsy Schwarzentraub

✝ O Master, let me walk with thee
in lowly paths of service free;
tell me thy secret; help me to bear
the strain of toil, the fret of care.

Teach me thy patience, still with thee
in closer, dearer company,
in work that keeps faith sweet and strong,
in trust that triumphs over wrong.

In hope that sends a shining ray
far down the future's broadening way,
in peace that only thou canst give,
with thee, O Master, let me live.

—Washington Gladden (1879)

✝ Read 2 Samuel 23:5.

In spite of the trials and tribulations of his life, as he came to the end, David was sure that he had served a God in whom he could place absolute trust. While David knew that he had not always been trustworthy, he knew even more surely that God had never broken the divine covenant with David and the people of Israel.

We need to know and trust this experience of God's love and forgiveness in our lives today. Personally, I must confess that when I face great adversity, danger, or hurt in my own life, and when I look to the future, I find it difficult to trust in the goodness of God's providence for me. When I am asked, "Do you believe in God's guidance and providence for your life?" I often respond, "In prospect I have difficulty, but as I look at my life in retrospect, I do firmly believe in the goodness of God's providence in my life."

As with David, after living three score years and ten, I have learned that you can trust God. God's word is always faithful. Though we often fail God, God never fails us. Sometimes it is our pain and suffering which enable us to hear the word of God and respond to the leading of God's Spirit.

Paul knew this when he penned the words in Romans 8:28: "And we know that all things work together for good for those who love God, who are called according to his purpose." Paul did not say that God is responsible for hurt or evil in our lives. But when we turn to God and place ourselves in God's hands, whatever our condition, God can and will work good in our lives. God's love and covenant with us is everlasting. We can count on that!

—Ira Gallaway

A Liturgy *for a* Prayer *or* Covenant Group Meeting

I. **Prayer of Invitation**
    God of all holiness and love, we invite your presence into our lives and into our gathering. Knit us together in mind and heart and lead us in faithfulness always. We pray in the strong name of Jesus. Amen.

II. **Hymn or Chorus**
    Choose one of the following:
    "Turn Your Eyes Upon Jesus" (*UMH* #349)
    "Kum Ba Yah" (*UMH* #494)
    "Jesus, Lover of My Soul" (*UMH* #479)
    "Jesus, Remember Me" (*UMH* #488)
    "Jesu, Jesu" (*UMH* #432)
    "Breathe on Me, Breath of God" (*UMH* #420)
    "On Eagle's Wings" (*UMH* #143)
    "Amazing Grace" (*UMH* #378)
    "Ask Ye What Great Things I Know" (*UMH* #163)
    "Draw Us in the Spirit's Tether" (*UMH* #632)

III. **Scripture Reading** (choose from these or select other scriptures)
    Matthew 18:15-20
    1 John 4:7-21
    Luke 18:35-43
    Romans 5:1-11
    Romans 3:21-31
    Romans 13:8-14
    1 Corinthians 1:8-31
    Colossians 1:9-14
    1 John 1:1-10

IV. **Silent Reflection**
    A time of silent reflection on the selection of the day. Use the questions below to guide your reflection.
    What is God saying to me through this passage?

What does this text prompt me to pray for?
What does this text prompt me to do?

V. **Mutual Sharing of Insights and Prompting**
Make certain every person has an opportunity to share his or her individual insight.
What common themes or promptings arise?
Are there insights we should explore further?
What action is suggested?
What are the directions for prayer?

VI. **Mutual Sharing of Concerns and Joys**
All of us carry joys and burdens. To share our joys is to multiply them. To share our concerns is to divide them as together we bear one another's burdens.
My joy today is . . .
My concern today is . . .

VII. **A Time of Mutual Prayer**
This time of prayer may include confession, petition, offering, and thanksgiving.
Silent prayer
Spoken prayer
The Lord's Prayer

VIII. **Next Steps**
What steps are we being led to take?

IX. **Prayer of Covenant**
Loving God, who keeps covenant with us, we offer ourselves anew to you in this hour. Do with us what you will, lead us where you will, send us to the task you will, and grant us grace to follow you more faithfully every day. In the name of Jesus. Amen.